CHRISTIANITY WITHOUT GOD

Moving beyond the Dogmas and Retrieving the Epic Moral Narrative

DANIEL C. MAGUIRE

Dev Publishers & Distributors
New Delhi

Published by
Dev Publishers & Distributors
Second Floor, Prakashdeep,
22, Delhi Medical Association Road,
Darya Ganj, New Delhi – 110 002

www.devbooks.co.in

ISBN 978-93-81406-48-9

This edition, 2015

Printed in India.

CHRISTIANITY WITHOUT GOD

To the American Association of University Professors
which stands tall as the defender of academic freedom and integrity.

CONTENTS

PART I

GOD

CHAPTER 1

OVERTURE

A Note on My Provenance

When I knelt on the marble floor of the chapel in Rome and heard the bishop intone over me, "Tu es sacerdos in aeternum" (you are a priest forever), I could never have imagined I would one day write this book. In these pages, I argue against the existence of a personal god, the divinity of Jesus, and the belief that continued living is the sequel to death. I find no persuasive arguments for any of those hypotheses.

The guiding maxim of my intellectual journey has been to follow the truth wherever it beckons.

My years as a professor have been almost exclusively in Catholic universities. I taught at Villanova University and at St. Mary's Seminary and University in Baltimore. I taught at the Catholic University of America, held the John A. O'Brien Chair in moral theology at the University of Notre Dame, and was visiting professor at Trinity College, Dublin. Most of my career has been at Marquette University, a Jesuit university in Milwaukee. I am past president of the Society of Christian Ethics. In 2014 that Society awarded me its Lifetime Achievement Award.

Early on I fell in love with the revolutionary moral classic that began with the mythopoetic Exodus/Sinai narrative and then pulsed like a building leitmotif through the maze of Hebrew and Christian scriptures and traditions.

In Parts I, II, and III of this book, I critique the Christian dogmatic triad of God, incarnation, and afterlife. In Part IV, I return to that brilliant moral epic often buried under corruption and dogmatic assertions of dubious epistemological pedigree. Much of this poetic classic is as piercingly relevant today as if it had been written this morning. It can take its place among other great moral classics, not as the best or last word but as a word that deserves a fresh hearing. It can speak again to our dangerous species' need to develop a realistic global ethic that can bring health to a planet deteriorating under the metastasizing effects of our ungrateful mismanagement.

Critique and Promise

It has long been assumed that Christianity rests on three foundational rocks: (1) a personal deity; (2) an incarnate divine Jesus who existed before his birth (as one in a trinity of divine persons); (3) continued living after death. I argue in this book that this dogmatic triad rests on fatal fault lines of cognitive instability and that these imaginative beliefs and hypotheses are more loosely rooted in biblical sources than is generally acknowledged. I further contend that these beliefs are not the best that Christianity can offer a troubled and troubling humanity.

Both theists and most of today's agitated atheists get a failing grade in literary criticism, the atheists by obsessing over the dogmas and the theists by mistaking metaphors for facts. Both miss the epic poetry that moves through the complex biblical literature.

In this book, I argue that the moral contribution of Christianity does not depend on the personal God and afterlife hypotheses, nor on doing to Jesus of Nazareth what Jesus did not do to himself—that is, turn him into a god. These beliefs, though comforting in some of their promises, are increasingly questionable. They suffer—all three of them—from (a) loose rootage in the Hebraic and Christian traditions; (b) falsely concretized metaphors and a reduction of poetic imagery to supposed historical and empirical facts; and (c) a century of scholarly research that has not been kind to the underlying assumptions of this dogmatic triad. This book critiques each of these dogmas on the basis of these weaknesses.

Properly understood and critiqued, the major religions are, at their best, classics in the art of cherishing, epics of revolutionary possibility-thinking—at least when they don't get mired in their own ebullient imaginations or get co-opted and pressed into service by the societal keepers of privilege and power. Because of the phantasmagoria religions generate, it is easy for secular minds to flail at them. From Feuerbach to Nietzsche, to the new mandarins of atheism, Hitchens, Harris et al., the tendency has been to bash the dogmas and ignore the moral wisdom and powerfully relevant insights into human psychology, politics, and, yes, economics, that these tainted classics carry in their poetic train.

Still, giving credit where credit is due, these vexed modern and postmodern critics of religion often argue well—and prevail—when they tilt their lances and charge. They do make many good points and are veritable hammers of noxious superstitions. Of course, they have an easy target. Impetuous religious imagination does run wild, providing a lot of grist for the mockery mill.

Religions Run Riot

We must face the fact that there is nothing that stirs the human imagination as much as the tincture of the sacred whether defined theistically or nontheistically. No area of literature produces the fantastical claims that religious literature does. From Jupiter to Kali the enigmatic Hindu goddess, from sexy gods who create with masturbation or intercourse to gods who create chastely with a simple word, from the extravagant gods of Sumer to the rambunctiously misbehaving gods of Olympus, from the African god who gets drunk on palm wine on his way to a botched creation to the more disciplined specialized gods who focus on agriculture or fertility or war, the *dramatis personae divinae* is endless. As the ancient Thales said, everything is full of gods and what a remarkable and idiosyncratic ensemble they are.

The gods of religious imagination are never static; they grow in talent and in tandem with the human species. With the invention of writing they turned to script, whether on tablets of stone at Sinai or by sending angels with names like Gabriel or Moroni to write books or leave hidden tablets. (There are as yet no divinely inspired films or videos, and no god is yet a Facebook friend.)

So there it is, a literature and a lore filled with gods and demigods and angels, with virgin births, resurrections from the dead, preexistence before conception (as some gospel writers, not all, allege for Jesus), and the ability to ascend into the skies without ever going into orbit. No literature can match religious literature in extravagances of imagination.

Religion's Flawed Immune System

In addition to exuberance run amuck, religion also invites critique and shunning because of its capacity for poison absorption. Religious thought is like a barometer, always sensitive and responsive to the surrounding atmosphere. Gentle peace-making ideas of the early Jewish and Christian movements imbibed violence in violent times and were transformed in harmful ways. Moral sicknesses become indentured and enshrined and are hard to cure because the faithful come to love them. When you are born into these dogmatic illnesses they seem as real as the starry sky above. When I was a young priest performing "the holy sacrifice of the mass," I did not feel that I was returning to the primitive penchant for human sacrifice. Yet on a daily basis, I offered the Father God his crucified bloodied son Jesus as a *hostiam sanctam*, a holy victim, in the hope this would lead to *salutis perpetuae*, "perpetual well-being." (The communion bread at the eucharistic meal is called *host*, from *hostia* meaning victim.) It was a reversion to the persistent ancient belief that the gods lust after sacrificial blood, with human blood being the preferred offering. I didn't know I was involved in a playing out of old myths redeployed to help explain the embarrassing scandal of Jesus' brutal execution.

Early eucharistic ceremonies did not center on the death of Jesus. In fact they often included dancing and were more marked by gratitude and hope rather than pathos. As Rita Nakashima Brock and Rebecca Parker discuss in their *Saving Paradise: How Christianity Traded Love of This World for Crucifixion and Empire*, the first crucifix showing the dead Jesus was not carved until the tenth century and images of Jesus' corpse were not found in churches before that ti. But violent times seeped in and rewrote the script and reshaped ι arts.

The results of this infusion of violent theology were and continue to be catastrophic for people and for this planet. Small wonder theologian Catherine Keller could write that theology "over its complex and conflictual history has legitimated more violence than any other ology."[2] Crusades, pogroms, and inquisitions come quickly to mind and they are still with us, though sometimes in camouflaged forms of prejudice and exclusion, often commingled with ethnic animosities.

Audiatur Altera Pars—Let the Other Side Be Heard

Understanding the positive moral content of religions is a daunting challenge, especially for the rationalistic mind. Reinhold Niebuhr wondered how an age so devoid of poetic imagination could ever understand religion and its poetry-rich literary products and rituals. Poetry, with its symbols and metaphors is disorienting to the hemmed-in rationalistic mind. Symbols are fearsome things. Like pregnancy and birthing, they stretch the skin of the complacent mind and leave permanent marks. But they are, like pregnancy, productive. The modern and postmodern mind is often dull when it comes to the wisdom of the heart, which is central to poetry and to one of its offspring, religion.

Art and religion were linked at their birth. As Karen Armstrong writes, even many rabbis, priests, and Sufis would say that "in an important sense God was a product of the creative imagination, like . . . poetry and music." Her research shows that "Men and women started to worship gods as soon as they became recognizably human; they created religions at the same time as they created works of art." Fear often engenders gods "to propitiate powerful forces" people did not understand. For many, theism functions as a kind of parental bulwark against meaninglessness and chaos; better fictive gods than a universe functioning without personalized divine oversight. Yet, as Armstrong says, there was more to the religious impulse: like art and philosophy, "these early faiths expressed the wonder and mystery that seem always to have been an essential component of the human experience of this beautiful yet terrifying world." Religion has always been "an attempt to find meaning and value in life."[3] It is the successes of that human quest that I attend to in Part IV of this book where I trace out the symphonic power of the morality narratives of the Hebrews and early Christians. I argue that that power is not organically linked to the theistic hypothesis.

Not all religion critics miss out on the positives of these symbolic movements. I would not list Richard Dawkins among the other "amateur atheists" of our day since he is aware of the philosophical and poetic richness that can be found in the creative efforts of religionists. Historically, the political-economic power of the Judeo-Christian moral vision won impressive praise from nontheistic social theorists. Friedrich Engels noted the revolutionary political power of early Christianity, a power that startled Diocletian and a number of emperors into harsh, repressive reaction. The threat was relieved only when Constantine was able to co-opt Christianity's subversive power. Engels spoke of Christianity as "the party of overthrow." He said it undermined not only the imperial religion but also "all the foundations of the state" by "flatly denying that Caesar's will was the supreme law." It pioneered a universalist, post-tribal mode of socialization. It was, Engels said, "international" and "without a fatherland." It had a "seditious" thrust that very quickly led to its suppression.

Engels went so far as to see the Christian movement as paradigmatic for socialism. Diocletian, he wrote, "promulgated an anti-Socialist—beg pardon, I meant to say anti-Christian—law." He runs on with the comparison noting that Christian symbols were forbidden "like the red handkerchiefs in Saxony" and that Christians were slowly banned from any effective participation in public life. He said the Christian revolution endured only for a time. Later it morphed into the state religion and lost the subversive power it inherited from prophetic Judaism.[4]

Lenin also compared the early Christian movement to the socialist revolt of the oppressed classes. (Both Engels and Lenin underestimate Christianity's debts to prophetic Judaism. Jesus, after all, was a Jew, not a Christian.) Lenin states that Marx's most fundamental teaching was that society should change from being "a democracy of the oppressors to the democracy of the oppressed classes." This hallmark of Marx's teaching, he laments, became "entirely forgotten" and was treated like "a piece of old-fashioned naiveté." He compares this lamentable defection to what befell Christianity. "Christians, after Christianity had attained to the position of a state religion, 'forgot' the 'naivetés' of primitive Christianity with its democratic-revolutionary spirit."[5]

Elaine Pagels says that the Christian emphasis on human equality was a breakthrough idea and an open defiance of totalitarianism. "Christians forged the basis for what would become centuries later, the western ideas of freedom and of the infinite value of each human life."[6]

But, again, in doing this, Christians were the heirs of prophetic Judaism. It was Jews, says Thomas Cahill, who were "the inventors of Western culture" since they freed themselves from the cyclical, *nihil sub sole novi* view of history, which made us prisoners of the past. They pioneered a vertical notion of history unlocking us from blind fate and opening us to possibility. Cahill goes so far as to suggest of this Jewish contribution "that it may be said with some justice that theirs is the only new idea that human beings have ever had."[7] It broke the chains of cyclical repetitiveness.

What Engels and Lenin saw, and what most Christians do not, is that the creative social and moral teaching of Judeo-Christianity is not tied to god-talk or to Christian afterlife hopes. Indeed afterlife hopes can relegate reforms to the postmortem bye-and-bye and sleight the rest of nature that enjoys no such otherworldly insurance backup. Modern Christians grouped under the "liberation" mantra do see the rich ores of progressive social theory that can be mined and appropriated from Hebraic and Christian sources and it is they—who really do get the point—who have so disquieted Vatican immobilists like Pope Benedict XVI. However, Benedict's successor Pope Francis is singing a new song—or actually an old one. He has returned to the revolutionary moral challenges treated in Part IV of this book and has repeatedly included atheists in his moral mission. In so doing he endorses the separability of theism from the biblical moral epic—no slight thing coming from a pope.

Distracted by God: Atheists and Theists United

Sad to tell, most modern atheists are as obsessed with "God" as the theists are. They are so busy *unbelieving* the dogmatic triad, and other dogmatic add-ons, that they miss the literary contributions housed in these human legacies. "Secular" scholarship generally tends to impose the violence of a prose reading on the poetry and symbolism of the religious traditions. This is less surprising when we note that none of the atheists *du jour* is a scholar in the field of religion. These fervent atheists join the faithful in reducing the infinitely varied and image-rich narratives and writings to a literal reading as though they were historical tracts or a kind of ancient journalism. Anti-poets take teachings like "exodus," "incarnation," and "resurrection" and downsize them, de-symbolizing them into happenings that could have been caught on film. When you mistake metaphor for fact, a metaphor like the virgin birth could have been verified by an OB/GYN attending physician.

Literalism Strips Metaphor Bare

Both atheists and theists mistakenly define religion as essentially a belief in one or usually more deities. I say "more" deities since the theistic impulse once indulged is not easily constrained to unicity. Even Christians with their avowed monotheism arrived at a "triune God" that sits uneasily on their one-God claims. No matter how hard the dons dunned, three never did equal one. Hinduism is crowded with multiple divinities and there is scant effort to find unicity at the base of its exuberant and densely populated pantheon. Islam is insistent on monotheism and yet, for some, the Qu'ran has the kind of status comparable to what orthodox Christians attribute to Jesus. Desecration of the Qu'ran is on a par with desecration of the consecrated eucharistic bread at a Catholic Mass. Deification is an impulsive penchant of our species and it is subject to mitosis. God-makers don't easily settle for just one.

But deity-centered religion leaves out a large portion of humankind whose religions do not believe in a deity or an afterlife. Chun-Fang Yu, a professor of Chinese religions says quite simply: "Unlike most other religions, Chinese religion does not have a creator god. . . . There is no god transcendent and separate from the world and there is no heaven outside of the universe to which human beings would want to go for refuge."[8] Instead, "The universe, or 'Heaven and Earth,' is the origin of everything, including human beings in the universe. This creating and sustaining force, otherwise known as the *Tao* or the Way, is seen as good and the highest goal of human life is to live in conformity to it."[9]

Atheists Defined by Their Opponents

Take note: Taoism, Confucianism, and Buddhism do not define themselves as "atheistic" since they don't entertain the theistic hypothesis as plausible and have no reason to define themselves in opposition to it as western atheists do. They don't need a negative definition of who they are and what they believe. And they can *believe* in human dignity and have *faith* in the power of human love without feeling that those words slide them into theism or some fanciful supernaturalism or life-after-death imaginings.

Western atheists are in the clumsy and defensive position of defining themselves with reference to what they do not believe, defined by their opponents. Small wonder that resentment suffuses their complaints. They must call themselves *unbelievers* to distance themselves from those who believe in a god and afterlife. Belief becomes a dirty word for atheists. There is an "Index of Forbidden Words" in their writing. Talk of the sacredness or sanctity of life is taboo since it is too redolent of god-talk for doctrinaire atheists. Western atheists suffer from an unnecessary limitation of language.

Religion as a Response to the Sacred

I offer in this book a definition of religion as *a response to the sacred, whether the sacred is understood theistically or nontheistically*. "Sacred" is simply the superlative of precious, the highest encomium we have to explain our peak experiences of value. Atheists need not cower before the word. It is not threatening to nontheistic Buddhists or

Taoists nor need it be to those who call themselves secular and who are not linked to any of the so-called major religions of the world. It is just a splendid superlative that need not be freighted with supernatural or preternatural baggage. There is no reason to be phobic about it. In a very practical sense it undergirds discussion of justice, law, and politics where "the sanctity of life" is the North star whether you are a theist or not.

The following graph illustrates some, not all, of the world's religions. Note that it includes agnostic/atheistic humanism. Secular humanists need not panic to find themselves in such company, on a graph of religion of all things! Those who reject the theistic hypothesis may have more of a sense of the sacred than do initiates of religions grown cold.

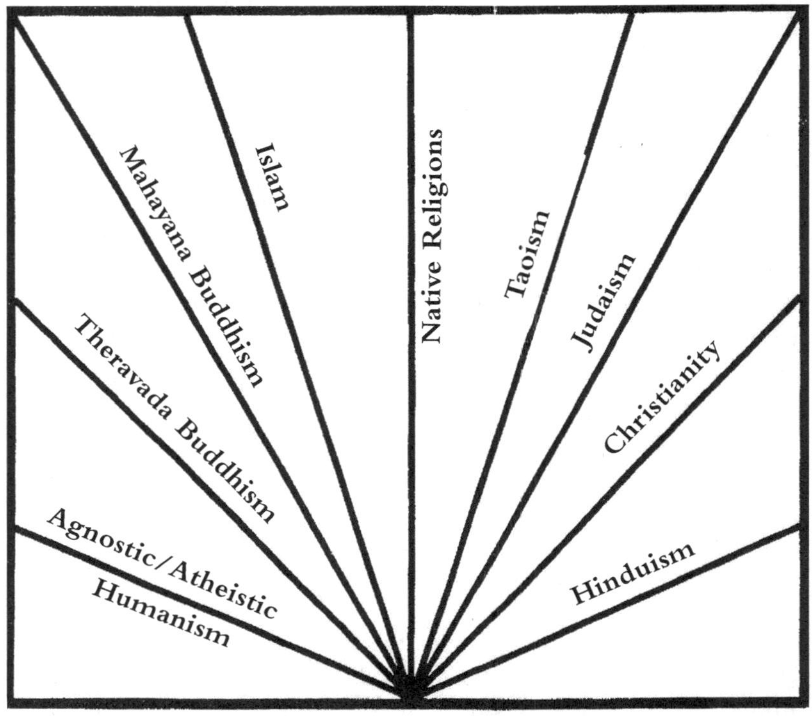

Model of Religions

Civilization is the offspring of awe. Alongside the horrors of the world—and the horrors of nature—we still see the first smiles of infants, the undefeatable growth of greenery from volcanic ash, the beauty of heroic love and great minds, the sunsets, the mallards, and the rose. We see all that and we say, "Wow!" However undignified the epithet, that Wow! is the birth-zone of moral awareness and the grounding of all humane living and law. I call it *the foundational moral experience.*[10] The ethical response pronounces the wonder of it all good; the religious response stretches for our highest compliment and calls it holy and sacred. This primordial awe breeds the "oughts" that blossom into laws and ensoul humane ethics, politics, and economics.

Notice, No God-Talk There. Not a Bit of It

It's humanity-talk, morality-talk. It is deeper than god-talk since god is but a fallible inference drawn by some from the wonder of it all. On god-talk the human race never has and never will unite. Indeed it is a perennial source of division and the world's "major religions" bear a formidable burden of proof that thus far in history they have done more good than harm. The worst of madmen, said the poet Alexander Pope, is a saint gone mad. But on the beauty of much of life and the "oughts" it inspires, we can all sit at the table, theists and nontheists alike, and share our experiences of appreciation. From such table-talk is civilization born.

The Separability of Dogmas and Morals

Chang Tsai (1020–1077), a major thinker in the Confucian tradition, produced what is seen as "a Confucian credo." It begins by saying that the earth and the universe are his father and mother:

> Therefore that which fill the universe I regard as my body and that which directs the universe I consider as my nature. All people are my brothers and sisters and all things are my companions. Show deep love toward the orphaned and the

> weak . . . and those who are tired, infirm, crippled, or sick; those who have no brothers or children, wives or husbands, all are my brothers who are in distress and have no one to turn to.[11]

Francis of Assisi would embrace every word of that credo. So, too, would Isaiah, Jeremiah, Hannah, and Jesus. The moral vision contained therein should not fall victim to unnecessary and futile disputes over a deity's existence or nonexistence, its unicity or multiplicity. When it comes to appreciating what we are and what we have in this privileged little corner of the universe, god-talk should not divide us. What would be refreshing is a moratorium on god-talk so that together we could explore alternatives to earth's current social, political, economic, and ecological distress.

CHAPTER 2

DEIFICATION

Religion and God: Who or What Are They Anyhow?

The atheists *du jour* are criticized for not being credentialed in religious studies or theology. In their defense it can be said that they have moved in to fill a void left by those who are professionals in the study of religion. Religious scholars should not feel slighted or put upon.

It is hard to be taken seriously when you are not sure who you are. Catherine Bell candidly reports that religion is "a field that is constantly resounding with litanies of alarm." It is "in trouble" because of its "crisis of identity," which makes "the professional study of religion muddled and uninfluential."[1] Robert Cummings Neville, in his presidential address to the American Academy of Religion, admits that the study of religion is in "crisis" when it comes to "self-definition."[2] That is no small crisis. Wilfred Cantwell Smith calls religion "notoriously difficult to define," noting that there is "a bewildering variety of definitions and no one of them has commanded wide acceptance."[3] J. W. Bowker sums it up: "Nobody seems to know what [religion] is."[4]

Compounding the confusion is the insistence on defining religion as theism rather than as *a response to the sacred* whether the sacred is theistically or nontheistically understood. Terms like *sacred* and *holy* express reverence for the wonder and beauty of life. They do not commit you to belief in gods or afterlife. Explaining religion in god terms is an arbitrary distraction from the experience of value that lies within terms like *the sanctity of life*, a term that is meaningful for theists and nontheists alike.[5] A definition of religion that leaves out god-talk can include nontheistic religions such as Taoism, Buddhism, and Confucianism.

Agnostic Theists

Beyond the confusion about the nature of religion, life gets even more trying for theists when they insist that the god they are talking about is actually unknowable. Augustine says you run into an epistemological brick wall if you even try to understand what or who God is. In talking about God, he said, if you claim to understand what you are talking about then what you have "understood" is not God. *Si comprehendis, non est Deus.*[6] Off-putting to say the least. Setting God outside the realm of the understandable or knowable is the very definition of agnosticism. Thomas Aquinas comments enigmatically and agnostically that the highest form of knowledge of God is the knowledge of God "as the unknown."[7] And again: "Now we cannot know what God is, but only what God is not; we must therefore consider the ways in which God does not exist, rather than the ways in which God does."[8] Agnostics and atheists, quizzically, and thoroughly baffled, would nod in agreement. Modern theologian Elizabeth Johnson adds to the befuddlement saying, "God is outside of all classes and categories and beyond the possibility of being imagined or conceived." Even Johnson calls this "a theological agnosticism more pervasive than has usually been acknowledged."[9] Point well taken. Very well taken indeed.

The Lubricity of "God"

History shows "God" as a slippery mutant. Karen Armstrong says the statement "I believe in God" has "no objective meaning, as such." Its meaning is derived from the constructions of believing communities. "If we look at our three religions [Judaism, Christianity, and Islam], it becomes clear that there is no objective view of 'God'; each generation has to create the image of God that works for it."[10] Armstrong says the same is true of atheists. They have to specify which conception of a deity they are denying.

The Apophatic Hideaway

Theists face a "damned if you do, damned if you don't" problem. They are painfully perched on the horns of a sharp dilemma: *anthropomorphism* or *agnosticism*. Anthropomorphism demotes god to sub-divine status. The deity is not very godly if god is just an upper case version of us. That leads to a dead end where you can't say anything intelligible about the deity, the prime subject of theistic religion. Say something intelligible and the transcendent "God" is gone. The word *apophatic* is brought forth to give a Grecian dress to this confusion. Apophatic is the cover for pious agnosticism. Apophatic means that it is best to bring negatives to god-talk so as not to shrink or de-divinize the deity down to human size. This is not a success story. Too many negatives compute to a cipher.

Denys the Areopagite commanded a lot of attention since he was supposed to be St. Paul's first Athenian convert, even though he was not. It's a sad way to go down in history, but he gets tagged by scholars as "Pseudo-Denys" since the real author is probably a sixth-century Greek writer. Denys, pseudo or not, saw the anthropomorphic trap and he went seriously apophatic. He didn't even like to use the word "god" since it was so humanly tainted. God, he said, was "above God," using the unusable word to recommend its nonuse. The unnameable is "a mystery beyond being." So very beyond being is the unnameable that it is "neither a unity or a trinity" and is best called "Nothing." The divinity is "not one of the things that are." Thinking about "God," according to Denys, is futile. "We have to leave behind us all our conceptions of the divine. We call a halt to the activities of our minds."[11] God-talk is a no-think zone.

Denys' pious nihilism traveled. The ninth-century Celtic philosopher Duns Scotus Erigena agreed with Denys that "God" cannot be said to exist because "God" is "more than existence." Faithful to Denys, Erigena says God is not something existing alongside other things. God "is" more, but then, sounding like Bill Clinton when he, too, was on the spot, Erigena said "what that 'is' is" cannot be defined. If we say God "is," we do not know what that "is" is.[12] He joins Denys in saying that God is best thought of as "Nothing." Theology, then, that is, the study of that which theological luminaries have described as an unknowable nothing, would seem open to charges of being nonsense, an elaborate but ill-fated effort to speak "effably" about the ineffable.

But even Job, in that hallowed book of the Bible, waxes apophatic.

> He passes by me, and I do not see him;
> he moves on his way undiscerned by me
> If I go forward, he is not there;
> if backward, I cannot find him;
> when I turn left, I do not descry him;
> I face right, but I see him not. (Job 9:11; 23:89)

Duns Scotus Erigena did have an insight worthy of his Celtic roots, and one that I defend. He said that theology is "a kind of poetry." He was on to it there. Poetry is where metaphors don't get reified, reduced to concrete things or persons, including *nothing-type-super-persons*. Poetry is the mind at its soaring imaginative best. It is mind as ecstatic, not apophatic. To that I will return.

Humpty Dumpty Semantics

Modern theologians are still enmeshed in linguistic contortionism. Hans Urs von Balthasar, a highly esteemed theologian, mounts what Elizabeth Johnson calls an "eloquent" defense of the "powerful incomprehensibility of the biblical God." (Apparently, incomprehensibility is graded on a scale from weak to powerful, with "God" having the powerful kind.) In an essay with an agnostic title, "The Unknown God," von Balthasar does not cringe in the face of the linguistic and numerical challenges presented by the "Triune God." God as "three" and yet also "one" is, in any calculus, confounding.

Not to worry, says von Balthasar "for what 'three' means in relation to the absolute is in any case something quite other than the inner worldly 'three' of a sequence of numbers."[13] God's "three" is not our three; it's a wholly other "three," unlike our worldly threes. (Maybe it's a one. Might it be a two?)

The comparison to Lewis Carroll's *Through the Looking-Glass* is inescapable. Humpty uses the word "glory" and tells Alice the word means "a nice knock-down argument." "But it doesn't mean that," protests Alice. "When I use a word," Humpty Dumpty insists scornfully, "it means just what I choose it to mean—neither more nor less." Alice the nonbeliever wonders "whether you can make words mean so many different things." Humpty's defense? "The question is which is to be master—that's all." And so, joining Humpty Dumpty, von Balthasar is master enough to say that the "three," which in earth-bound talk means one more than two and one less than four, really doesn't mean any of that in god-talk. There it means whatever theologians choose it to mean, nothing more, nothing less. So, in summary, in holy mathematics, when it comes to "God" who is best thought of as the unknowable nothing, three does not equal three, nor does "is" mean "is."

Insisting that God is incomprehensible and yet must be talked about inevitably leads into double-talk. Cynthia Crysdale and Neil Ormerod address "mostly incomprehensible ideas (like God . . .)." They then insist that "incomprehensible does not necessarily mean unintelligible."[14] But, wait! If the deity is "mostly incomprehensible," then it must be a little teeny bit comprehensible. Then that teeny bit would be intelligible and describable like other knowable things, and that old bugaboo anthropomorphism has again slipped like a camel's nose into the tent of god-talk.

Escape Routes

Humphrey Palmer cites the problem of theologians who speak of God as "totally different, but . . .": "If theologians use words in their ordinary sense, then theology will be anthropomorphic. If, on the other hand, a term is to mean something quite different when applied to God, then theology is incomprehensible."[15] At this point, a practical conclusion suggests itself. When it comes to god-talk, don't do it. "Just say no" to god-talk. That's what the Book of *Esther* did in the Bible; it just dropped the god-talk. Esther, sadly, was not a trendsetter.

Theists, however, eventually gag on their own agnosticism. Their apophatic zeal runs thin. And so it comes to pass that these same theologians who stoutly deny anything you can say, think, or imagine about God, do a stunning *volte face* and sally forth speaking of God in fervently understandable terms: as lover, friend, parent, lawgiver, conversation partner, and all kinds of other quite comprehensible things. The unimaginable is imagined and given distinct functions, gender, personality traits, and a major role in history.

In popular piety, moreover, the apophatic doesn't fly. Anthropocentrism reigns. There are no apophatic pews in churches. (Even in the National Football League the deity is engaged and thanked for touchdowns and invoked by the sign of the cross before an attempted field goal. The last thing the field goal kicker needs is a "Nothing" god whose threes might only be a one.)

Whither do beleaguered theists go for release from this bind? They seek out three paths to salvation, each of them thick with brambles and pitfalls: *revelation, analogy*, and *abstraction*.

The Bible

The Bible is held to be the revealed "word of God," so it is clearly the first stop in the quest for meaningful god-talk. Maybe biblical revelation can get us off the horns of that daunting dilemma. Theologian Johnson is hopeful: "Revelation gives certain key images of God not attainable though natural reason, as well as the gift of a clearer intellectual light by which to understand them."[16] That is both promising and weird, a kind of supernatural knowledge the human mind could never have come up with on its own. Johnson admits that this revelation, endowed as it is with insights inaccessible to reason, still leaves us "united to God as to an unknown." Now this is a major letdown. Apparently that "clearer intellectual light by which to understand" is not very bright and does not banish agnosticism. (One is inclined to cry out again, where is Esther when we need her? After all, even though Esther dropped the god-talk she still made it into the Bible.)

God-talk in the Bible does not achieve symphonic cohesion. The gods that appear in the Bible seem to be cultural artifacts, with discernible lineage in the history of the people who created them. All the gods seem to vindicate the ancient and cynical Xenophanes who said that if horses and cattle did theology the gods of the horses would be equine and the gods of the cattle would emerge in the image and likeness of cattle. Gods are *ex cultura*, not *ex nihilo*. Gods also are usually amalgamations of other godly predecessors. So the Egyptian religion had Osiris and Serapis. When Greek imperialists sought some unity with their Egyptian subjects in a bit of tactical ecumenism, they fused Osiris with the Greek god Apis, calling the hybrid Oserapis, and eventually simply Serapis. The Babylonian god Marduk also illustrates the hybrid nature of the gods. "Mesopotamian major gods got swallowed up by Marduk, one by one."[17] Marduk simply assumed all the roles that the other gods had as specialties, everything from rainmaking to accounting. No god, including Yahweh, escaped this syncretistic identity-formation process. It is not surprising that Yahweh, like other divine hybrids, would suffer from multiple personality disorder. They all do.

The Bible's "God" is a work in progress, a work that never gets completed. As Robert Wright says: "If you read the Hebrew Bible carefully, it tells the story of a god in evolution, a god whose character changes radically from beginning to end."[18] The god we get, as Jack Nelson-Pallmeyer writes, is a "composite deity with many characteristics of neighboring gods and religions."[19] Jack Miles puts it simply: "The God whom ancient Israel worshiped arose as the fusion of a number of the gods whom a nomadic nation had met in its wanderings."[20] Osmosed into this god's corporate personality we find many antecedents such as Baal, Tiamat, Marduk, and others. More alarming yet, the Hebrew Bible's god was not a monotheist. According to the Book of Exodus, Yahweh was a deity among deities. "Who is like thee, O lord, among the gods?" (5:11). Yahweh was jealous about his divine identity. He needed to be, according to the Bible, because he was not the only god in town. But he was the best: "the Lord your God is God of gods, and Lord of lords" (Dtr. 10:17), more "great and mighty" compared to the other competing divinities. Those other gods were a constant concern and the people needed to be repeatedly warned against their allures.

In no slight irony, even the Ten Commandments, which conservative Christians want to post in American courthouses, take the existence of other gods for granted and warn the people against them in the very first Commandment (Ex. 20:2). Again, Karen Armstrong: "It is very difficult to find a single monotheistic statement in the whole of the Pentateuch."[21] (Noteworthy, too, is the fact that those Commandments also mention slavery as an acceptable practice. [Ex. 20:8–11].)

Good God, Bad God

Israel's God is presented in a rich literary imagery, anthropomorphic to the core. God walks in the garden in the cool of the day, gets worn out from his creative labors and takes a day off to rest. God has a warm and compassionate side. He cares for "widows and orphans and loves the immigrant who lives among you, giving him food and clothing" (Dtr. 10:18–19). Isaiah lauds all that the Lord has done "in his tenderness by his many acts of love." He saves people "by his love and pity, lifting them up and carrying them though all the years" (Isa. 63:7–10). Psalm 100 tells us "the Lord is good; his mercy is everlasting." And yet Leviticus shows this same Lord taking a violent, demoniacal turn, ordering us to slaughter our disobedient children as well as adulterers and those who engage in same-sex coupling. If a priest's daughter becomes a sex worker, "she shall be burnt to death" (21:19). There is a Jekyll in the biblical God, and there is also a Hyde.

Still on the downside, this morally bifurcated god is also capable of brutal bias and favoritism. Israel was the apple of his eye, preferred before all others. This is not good news for other nations who must be subordinated to Israel's interests. Isaiah makes it clear:

> Your gates shall always be open;
> day and night they shall not be shut,
> so that nations shall bring you their wealth,
> with their kings led in procession.

For the nations and kingdoms
that will not serve you shall perish;
those nations shall be utterly laid waste. (60:11–12)

To guarantee Israel's dominance, this God who urged compassion becomes a "warrior" (Ex. 15:1) and a ruthless disciplinarian. If Israel does not obey God's command, God will "pile your rotting carcasses on the rotting logs that were your idols, and I will spurn you . . . you shall eat your sons and your daughters. . . . I will make your cities desolate and destroy your sanctuaries. . . . I will destroy your land, and the enemies who occupy it shall be appalled. . . . I will pursue you with the naked sword; you land shall be desolate and your cities heaps of rubble" (Lev. 26:27–34). Clearly he was not one to spare the rod. When Jerry Falwell and Pat Robertson were scorned for their belief that the 9/11 massacres and the reduction of the Twin Towers to "heaps of rubble" were the work of an angry God, they were not out of tune with many parts of the Bible.

When Jephthah was filled with "the spirit of the Lord," it didn't speak well for the Lord or his spirit. Jephthah swore that if he was successful at slaughtering the Ammonites and others he would sacrifice the first person to come out of the door of his house after his victory as a "whole-offering" to the Lord. Who was the first person to come out the door to meet him "with tambourines and dances but his daughter, and she his only child." She begged for two months to "roam the hills with my companions and mourn that I must die a virgin." He allowed that and then sacrificed her to fulfill his vow to the Lord (Judg. 11:29–40). The Hebrew and Christian scriptures paint a God who manifested unstinting love on the one hand and sociopathic behavior on the other.

The last word of the Bible, the Christian *Book of Revelation*, shows Bad God at his worst. The heavens open and there is the Lord, his eyes flaming "like fire . . . robed in a garment drenched in blood. He was called the Word of God and the armies of heaven followed him on white horses. . . . From his mouth there went a sharp sword with which to smite the nations; for he it is who shall rule them with an iron rod, and tread the winepress of the wrath and retribution of God the sovereign Lord" (Rev. 19:11–16). Small wonder the conclusion of Jack Nelson-Pallmeyer that "Jesus dies in order to save us from God, not from sin . . . [to save us] from a violent God who punishes sin."[22] This is consistent with the Hebrew scriptures. Regina M. Schwartz argues that the "sacrifices of Cain and Abel suggest . . . an offering to ward off divine wrath."[23] The problem of god as solution and god as menace is never resolved in the biblical stories.

Analogy to the Rescue

Analogy is the next defense against the terrible Sophie's Choice of a god who is too human to be credibly divine and a god who needs to be somewhat knowable to be of any use at all. Paul, who thrived on overstatement, says knowledge of "God" is no problem: "All that may be known of God by people lies plain before their eyes; indeed God himself has disclosed it to them. His invisible attributes, that is to say his everlasting power and deity, have been visible, ever since the world began, to the eye of reason, in the things he has made." There is therefore "no possible defense" for those who say they know not "God" (Rom. 1:18–21). This text has been the capstone of the analogists. The analogical approach says that god, incomprehensible though he be, is still the creator of all we know. Shadows of the cause are always discernible in the effects. Created reality reflects uncreated reality, that is, god. We make cognitive contact with the *invisbilia* through the *visiblia* of our created world.

Fortified with the disclaimer that the analogically known god is not *really* known, the back door is opened to an anthropomorphic avalanche of names and functions that are now applicable to the unknowable "God." This indirectly, analogically glimpsed God is again talked of in the most familiar down-home anthropomorphic of terms such as: lover, friend, parent, lawgiver, conversation partner, judge, shepherd, farmer, laundress, potter, fisherman, midwife, merchant, physician, artist, nurse, metal worker, and homemaker. And gender is no longer a problem since analogy gives *carte blanche* to our image-making. Male, female, hermaphroditic . . . it matters not a whit since it is all analogical anyhow; it's not the real thing because the real thing has been dogmatically declared to be incomprehensible. Through analogical sleight-of-hand, the unknowable god is known, and Humpty Dumpty has survived his fall and rides again. In the background of the analogical chorus we hear echoes from the topsy-turvy world where "three" is not three and "is" is not is.

Analogy thus used is a trick play that offends sound epistemology. The fundamental problem with the analogy bypass is that *analogy only works among comprehensibles.* Analogy illumines the less obvious by looking to the better known and more obvious. It assumes knowability. It cannot help you *know* what you have already proclaimed as utterly unknowable. Analogists, clinging to both ends of this oxymoron say in self-defense: "Analogy means likeness, and God is like all those things, but not really, in fact, not at all." "Not at all" says it all. We're back to "nothing" talk. "Not at all" is the epitaph of the analogy gambit.

Compartmentalizing the Bad God

Jewish, Christian, and Muslim theists manage to ignore the Bad God as though he were an embarrassing relative. He is not invited to family reunions. It is the Good God who presides at their Thanksgiving dinners. This is not surprising since an "all powerful and merciful God" is useful. He can meet humanity's greatest needs. The most pressing human need is security from chaos, and here, a benign, omnipotent deity could deliver. The nineteenth-century Vatican Council leaned on the Bible (Wisd. 8:1) to express the god-solution to the threat of meaninglessness. "God in his providence, protects and guards everything he created, as he orders all things benignly (*suaviter*) with his unquestionable power (*fortiter*)." The Council also adds the reassurance that all things are naked and open to this god's eyes including the future.[24] Such a god would seem a panacea for our deepest anxieties and a refuge from all uncertainty.

Still, *fortiter* and *suaviter* are not descriptive of the view from the Hubble telescope nor are they favored by modern cosmology, which says that our rather orderly planet is on a brief (in cosmic terms) holiday from the chaos that spawned it and to which it shall return in the apocalyptic tumult that is our planetary destiny. Stardust we were and unto stardust we shall return. From that cosmic fate no metaphoric god shall save us. The alleged designer of this current terrestrial order designed it to fail. It, like we, will die.

Morality and God-Talk

Whatever the travails of the god-talk people, secularists need to remember that god-talk is always pregnant. Ignore it at your peril since it houses people's deepest convictions. A study entitled *Religion, the Missing Dimension of Statecraft* chronicles a series of errors in American statecraft caused by ignoring religious influences on international affairs and political behavior.[25]

God-talk mirrors culture, so even the horrors of the Bad God are lessons in human moral pathology. Beyond that, as I argue, a penetrating morality narrative is present in the Bible and the traditions it inspired and spawned. It is a narrative that attains to classical excellence with the "perpetual contemporaneity" that marks a true classic; there is more to god-talk than talk of god. Such is the way of metaphor. Much that is symbolized by the Good God illumines that morality narrative. If you are phobic about religion-talk you can miss a lot. If you take god-talk literally you miss the poetry and that poetry as I argue in Part IV is replete with creative envisioning and down-to-earth insights. There are ideas there that should require no passport to enter an open mind.

The Abstract and Neutered God Solution

Theologian John F. Haught tries with great subtlety to redesign the known-but-unknown God problem. He recognizes that if we personalize god and give him or her gender, anthropomorphism is the winner and the transcendent "God" is no more. He accepts the tradition that says "God" is "unavailable, "unverifiable," "hidden," and he refers to the "scandal" of divine hiddenness. He is blunt and spot-on in stating that believers would have trouble "surrendering to something that is less intense in being than they are, that is, to something that does not have at least the stature of personality (which is the most intense form of being of which we have any direct experience)."[26] He avoids debates over "God's" gender and prefers thinking of "God" as "neuter." His book is entitled not *who* but *What Is God*. He sees God's reality as best illumined through abstract concepts such as "depth, future, freedom, beauty, and truth." This neutering of divinity he sees as "a necessary corrective to a one-sidedly personalistic understanding."[27]

However well intentioned this intellectual effort, the neutered god will not play well in the pews. The folks in the temple, mosque, or church demand "a one-sidedly personalistic" god. They don't direct their prayers to "depth, future, freedom, beauty, and truth." They are talking to somebody, not ruminating about noble abstractions.

The same can be said of Gordon D. Kaufman's thinking of "God" as "serendipitous creativity." Kaufman, like Haught, admits the theist's known/unknown dilemma. "God is, in the last analysis, utterly unknowable." We must not "reify" god in any way or "think that we really know what or who God is."[28] His preferred abstraction is "serendipitous creativity." Once again we have neutering and another flight from personalized god-talk. By moving from personalized god-talk to "the metaphor of creativity," Kaufman notes that it brings us into closer conversation with Buddhist, Taoist, and Confucian views of reality. Since those views are, in the main, nontheistic, Kaufman's approach does seem to be sliding directly onto the path to a nontheistic Christianity.

Serendipitous creativity is not yet on church banners nor do we look for it carved in stone on Cathedral doors. It will not be spelled out in gilded mosaic above the high altar. Neither will we find Tillich's "ground of being" displayed in devotional shrines. Christians claim an incarnate God, which—let it be conceded—is the last word in anthropomorphic thinking. "Serendipitous creativity" does not become incarnate, have siblings, eat fish, and drink wine and even be accused of overindulging. Surely the work of Haught and Kaufman is fascinating theory but it is not real god-talk. The Bible shoots it down in its opening words when it says that "in the beginning" a hard-working anthropomorphic god did it all and had to rest up afterward.

Bishop John Shelby Spong also takes the abstractionist turn but with some curious twists. Spong makes statements that would be at home in traditional orthodoxy. "I believe passionately in God . . . in the reality of God." "I do not argue for a moment that God is not real. Indeed, the reality of the god-experience overwhelms me every day of my life."[29] He talks the language of analogy, looking for "God's footprints," going where he perceives "that God has been." "We visualize and experience God's effects, not God's being."[30] Spong does pay his apophatic dues, saying that God "by definition, lies outside the capacity of the human mind."[31] "God is not a supernatural entity." But then the bishop speaks with forked tongue in a chapter entitled "Beyond Theism But Not Beyond God."[32] He insists that theism and deism are dead but God is not. His is a "nontheistic God."

Time to bring on the abstractions: "God is love . . . God is Being . . . God is life."[33] One can speak of love, life, and being without bringing God into it with no loss whatever. To avoid anthropomorphism, Spong takes the step other abstractionists avoid. He takes on prayer. This is the ultimate test for the abstractionists. Is there a personal deity one can talk to in prayer and worship? Sorry, says Spong, but there is not. "Prayer perpetuates the primary illusion of theism—namely, that we are not alone, that there is a personal power somewhere, which is greater than the limited power of humanity, and that this personal power can effectively deal with all of those issues that lie beyond human competence to solve."[34] We need to get over the idea of prayers "as adult letters to Santa Claus." Spong is clear that "prayers of petition" will be marked *Return to Sender: No Such Person at This Address.*

Some other meaning of prayer must be found. Prayer is not talking to someone since there is no super-someone to talk to. Prayer might mean something, he says, if it means "meditation" or "contemplation" or "breathing exercises that are designed to heighten self-awareness."[35] Nontheistic Buddhists would have no trouble with anything Spong says about living lovingly and compassionately with growing mindfulness and self-awareness, but they would have no need of Spong's "God"-talk. Nor does he. He clings to the "God" word as the bereaved cling to mementoes of the dearly departed dead. Better the realism of Thomas Cahill, who while writing brilliantly of the positives in Judaism and Christianity, admits matter-of-factly "it cannot be proven that God exists."[36]

Closeted Agnostics

When Catholic theologian Elizabeth Johnson speaks of "a theological agnosticism more pervasive than has usually been acknowledged," it can be said on close inspection that the agnosticism is peeking through. Gary Gutting is professor of philosophy at the University of Notre Dame and editor of *Notre Dame Philosophical Reviews*. He is a product of eight years of teaching by Ursuline nuns and of twelve more years by Jesuits. He still identifies himself as a believing Catholic. Yet he says, "as to the theistic metaphysics, I'm agnostic about it taken literally." His reference is to the traditional Catholic arguments for the existence of God. While agnostic about these arguments, he sees them "as a superb intellectual construction that provides a fruitful context for understanding how our religious and moral experiences are tied to the ethics of love." (The "ethics of love" can thrive and does so in other moral traditions without reference to Catholic metaphysical arguments for the existence of a personal deity.) He sees "the historical stories" of Christianity "as parables illustrating moral and metaphysical teachings." That would seem to include such "historical stories" as resurrection, ascension, and parthenogenesis. He does not see the views of the hierarchy as controlling, especially their "rigid strictures on sex and marriage." Professor Gutting acknowledges that such a position may seem better described as "ultra liberal Protestant" or "Unitarian." He does not shrink from these charges but avers "that Catholicism, too, has reconciled itself to the Enlightenment view of religion." None of this would pass muster at Nicaea or Chalcedon or in the upper levels of today's Vatican. Still, Gutting finds in Catholicism his creedal home.[37]

Garry Wills, in his *Why Priests?: A Failed Tradition*, rejects the idea of a priesthood, a papacy, and a eucharist, and yet he still counts himself among his "brothers and sisters in Christ of the Roman persuasion."[38] "Cafeteria Catholic" refers to Catholics who pick and choose what they believe. Wills brings this selective freedom to a whole new level. What we see in writers such as Gutting and Wills is Catholicism in the process of being redefined.

Robert W. Funk, one of the founders of the Jesus Seminar where biblical scholars seek out what can truly be said about Jesus of Nazareth, says that the term *God* needs quotation marks around it, so uncertain is its meaning. "I hesitate to call Jesus' faith a faith in 'God,' since when we use the term 'God' these days, we find it necessary to put quotation marks around it to indicate how problematic the term has become." Regarding the status of Jesus he says: "Jesus himself should not be, must not be, the object of faith. That would be to repeat the idolatry of the first believers." The problem, as he sees it, is that "the history of Jesus the man has been smothered by the myth of the Christ." Of contemporary Christianity he says: "Christianity as we have known it in the West is anemic and wasting away." Only radical reform and "a rescission of many traditional elements" can reform it and give it a future.[39]

Not all the agnosticism among Christian scholars admitted by theologian Elizabeth Johnson is staying in the closet, though that closet is by no means empty.

Can Jesus Help?

Ironically, Jesus himself is a huge problem for Christians who want a transcendent non-anthropomorphic deity. From what we know of him, Jesus did not buy into a god hidden in abstractions. His god was not neuter but was clearly anthropomorphic and gendered. "Abba, Father," Jesus called him, the affectionate, very personal term for father in Aramaic (Mark 14:36). Jesus prayed and he did not ask the "ground of being" for our daily bread. He did not quibble about what "is" is, nor did he engage the mathematical challenge of trying to prove that three equals one.

The very concept of "revelation" is as anthropomorphic as Jesus. "Religions of the book," Judaism, Christianity, and Islam, posit a talking deity, talking as *anthropoi* do. And Nicaea's *homoousios* decision made anthropomorphism official church doctrine. *Anthropos* and *theos* were solemnly declared to be *of one and the same being*. Theism's unavoidable oxymoron shined bright at Nicaea and in the creeds of all its conciliar sequels. And to that I will return.

Indeed, Kaufman's serendipitous creativity would serve better as a synonym for "natural selection," which also addresses the problem of how everything came to be, and to that I return. Serendipitous creativity well describes what we do know about the evolutionary process. There is a creative thrust in nature and laws that extend from here to the quasars. There is often fossil evidence of the adaptive serendipitous creativity of this still unfolding mysterious process. But those who work on natural selection face what they do not know as a challenge not as a dead end. They do not divinize the unknown. They keep working at it.

Theism, looked squarely in the face, is a pessimistic agnosticism. Faced with the unanswered questions of evolution, theism throws up its hands and says X did it, and then falls down and worships X—insisting all the while that the X that did it all and gives us the final answer is beyond our ken and, in fact, is best called "nothing."

In nuce, my argument is that the question "Does God exist?" is a flawed question, undermined by its own assumptions.

CHAPTER 3

PROLIFERATION

Gods as Hybrids: E Pluribus Unum

Scratch a god and find a need. God-talk rises from perceived needs and the concerns those need engender. The functions of the gods give it away. In the second millennium BCE the ancient Mesopotamian scribes gave us no fewer than 2,000 named gods. They were functionally distinguished. Obviously the weather gods were everywhere in antiquity and so sun, moon, and storms had gods defined by these essentials of life. But as life developed, new gods were created to handle humanity's new capacities. Historically, nature gods were phase one since we stood in terrible awe of these forces we could not understand or control. But then we began to get some control over nature by the beginning of the Upper Paleolithic age when, as Arnold J. Toynbee said, we began to improve our "previously almost static technology."[1] As we started to cultivate plants and domesticate animals, we assigned gods to preside over these new human enterprises. Eventually there were gods for farmers, brewers, merchants, brick-makers, and craftsmen. There were also gods for robbers and sex-workers. (Resonance of this can be found in modern sex workers in Latin American with Christian symbols on their bed table.)

The metaphoric nature of god-making shows through especially in the transmogrification of gods from one role to another and in their sex-change operations. We had gods for water, vegetables, and the wind. Specific vegetables that had a centrality of need got their own divine patron, such as Athena the olive goddess. But then life changed and the gods changed with us. Humans were impressed with their sensational victories over nature such as "the conversion of the once-savage jungle-swamps in the lower Tigris-Euphrates valley and in the lower Nile valley into docile canals and dykes and fields."[2] Productivity increased as did population. We moved from simple neolithic villages to the complexity of a Sumerian city-state. The nature gods who had served their purpose then got called into higher service. More precisely, they kept their old jobs and got new ones. They underwent a kind of identity transplant. While still representing the natural forces, they were now called on also to represent and sacralize political communities.

Enlil the wind-god became the deification of the state of Nippur. Nanna the moon-god did the same service for the state of Ur. This process continued in what we call somewhat prematurely *civilization.* Athena the olive-goddess became the deification of the state of Athens, and with a slight name change, also the deification of Sparta. Poseidon the water-god deified Corinth. Baal became the Tyre god. "The volcano-god or thunder-god Yahweh is the deification of the states of Israel, Judah, and Edom. The local communities have become divinities, and these divinities that stand for collective human power have become paramount over the divinities that stand for natural forces." Toynbee adds this cautionary observation that still has application to our day, saying "the injection of this amount of religious devotion into nationalism has turned nationalism into a religion, and this a fanatical one."[3] He opines that "nationalism is 90 percent of the religions of 90 percent of the people of the Western world and of the rest of the world as well."[4]

Godly Sex Change

When Leonard Shlain visited ancient shrines in Greece, he kept encountering shrines that at first had been dedicated to female deities but in almost every case had been reconsecrated to a male deity. This sex-change went beyond Greece. At one time, male gods held sway when hunting was job one and those gods were of the macho type, bold and courageous. But, agriculture changed all of that and the goddess rose to ascendancy. The Mother Goddess appeared under many names: Inanna in Sumer, Isis in Egypt, Asherah in Syria, Astarte in Greece, and Aphrodite in Cyprus. The male consorts of the female goddesses were weak and subordinate sorts.

Writes Shlain: "For several thousand years, every people throughout the Fertile Crescent venerated a deity who personified the Great Goddess. When we speak of this area as the 'cradle' of civilization, we tacitly acknowledge the superior mold the feminine principle played in the 'birth' of modern humankind."[5] Gender, however, was very unstable with the gods. The Mother Goddess was dethroned. And when the goddesses fell, the status of women generally fell with them. "Around 1500 BCE there were hundreds of goddess-based sects enveloping the Mediterranean basin. By the fifth century CE they had been almost completely eradicated, by which time women were also prohibited from conducting a single major Western sacrament. . . . The systematic political and economic subjugation of women followed."[6] God-talk is never unrelated to the facts on the ground, the political and economic facts.

The sociology of knowledge would have no trouble explaining this. Things happening on the ground were shaping the shaping of the gods, and the gods were very accurately reflecting life situations. Social analysis that ignores god-talk is impaired in its reality contact. The metaphoric constructed nature of god-talk lends insight into social realities. God-talk is not only a quest for the *deus faber*, the creator who is the answer to the question "who done it?" regarding the origins of the earth. God-talk is also an answer to the question "who are we?"

As the Jesuit Indian theologian Ignatius Jesudasan puts it: "Every image that has ever been projected of God is a mirror reflecting the age and person or group which produced it."[7] He adds: "Religions themselves are but metaphorical names and forms of ethnic societies."[8] Nations and their gods are consanguineous. And our nations still continue to meld into gods. This explains the fervor of nationalism and the pious esteem for "the supreme sacrifice," the offering of one's life for the State seen at the height of nobility. Religious symbols, crosses and Stars of David, adorn the graves of dead soldiers. As Jurgen Moltmann says, since the time of Constantine, the "Christian martyr" was turned into "the Christian soldier." "The crown of the martyr was changed into the medal of honor for bravery and victory. In this way, the death of the soldier receives a religious halo" and becomes "sanctified."[9]

The secularization process is not as advanced as seculars are wont to think.

God as Time-Traveler and Mutant Metaphor

Theologian and poet Catherine Keller makes a point often ignored by theologians. There are only two definitions of "God" in the Bible and neither one defines "God" as an entity, much less a person. The two are: "God is spirit" (John 4:24) and "God is love"(1 John 4:8).[10] In the latter text, knowing God is not like knowing persons or things. "Everyone who loves . . . knows God" (1 John 4:7). This moves "knowledge of God" out of propositional knowledge with its clumsy apophatic disclaimers—and redefinition of words—into a symbolic realm. This actually brings god-talk close to theologian John Haught who brought "beauty" and "truth" to the fore in trying to understand what god-talk is all about. But it does not support the theism of Christian orthodoxy, which posits a very personal and active deity.

The Bible, did not linger in this abstract vein, nor did John, the Evangelist, stick with it. Anthropomorphism triumphed. From its early polytheism the Bible struggled toward a more spiritualized monotheism, a goal it never fully attained.

Monotheism had a rough launching in the Bible. The goddess Asherah was worshipped alongside Yahweh in Solomon's Temple for most of its existence, for 236 out of 370 years. As Rosemary Radford Ruether says, Judaism did not expunge all "reminiscences of a male-female *pleroma* (community of persons in the divine).[11] Arnold J. Toynbee observed: "Pre-Christian Judaism had even relaxed the rigidity of its monotheism so far as to associate with its One and Indivisible God a Word and a Wisdom which . . . had come near to anticipating the Second and Third Persons of the Christian Trinity in Unity."[12]

Christians, after the canon of the Bible was closed, hewed out their mathematical anomaly and gave us three persons equaling one deity. The Bible can't be blamed for the triune God. As Oxford University's Dennis Nineham says, the doctrine of the Trinity and the Incarnation are "essentially patristic constructions."[13] The Bible, says Nineham, does not offer "conclusive argument" for "the objective existence of three distinct divine hypostases such as are presupposed in traditional trinitarian teaching."[14] This lack of biblical footing did not deter the proliferators and the triune God was ensconced into orthodoxy.

The Perils of Travel

Three things happened as "God" took off into Christian history: (1) Christian thinkers struggled to find a way to think of God in nonmaterial, noncorporeal terms; (2) God's personality kept changing, often in ways that mocked the biblical promise that "God is love"; (3) polytheism returned hale and hearty.

First, in the first century BCE, there was movement in Israel toward spiritualizing God. It was a hard sell. Even as late as Augustine in the fifth century CE, the idea of a spiritual rather than material God was not prevalent. Spiritualizing God was necessary because if God was to be presented as eternal and immutable, as philosophically minded Christians desired, bodiliness would get in the way. As Jesuit philosopher Roland J. Teske writes, "until the time of Augustine there simply was not present in the Western Church a concept of the spiritual in the sense of a non-corporeal substance."[15] For a number of years, Augustine believed "that the Catholic Church held that God was in the form and shape of a human being." For a long time, Augustine conceived of "God" as a material substance, "an immense shining body" and a "vast corporeal mass."[16]

He was not alone in this. Tertullian (160–225) said that what is not material does not exist: "*Nihil est incorporale nisi quod non est.*" Then he took the oxymoronic plunge saying that "God" is a body even if he is a spirit: "*Quis negabit Deum corpus esse, etsi Deus spiritus est?*" Augustine finally settled on the idea of "God" as "a spiritual substance."[17] Amid the maze of such oxymorons—and such strained nominalism—one is permitted to wonder what if anything is being said here.

Second, as Christian history unfolded, the good god took a mean turn. In his study of medieval Christianity in the ninth and tenth centuries, Dennis Nineham chronicles how theology managed to turn its god into a savage ogre. The influential Augustine bore a lot of guilt—not all—for this sick vision of reality. The collective guilt narrative was this: Adam and Eve sinned, preferring the Devil's counsel to God's. As a result of this primeval sin, the entire human race became a *massa perditionis*, a damned mass of people all sharing in the guilt of their original ancestors. We were thus born guilty and deserving of the ultimate punishment. As Nineham says: "This meant that simply to be born was to be hell-worthy and that the eternal damnation of even the youngest un-baptized baby was fully justified."[18] Some lucky people could be saved, but that was by the unmerited mercy of their god. As few as one in a thousand might be saved.[19] Signaling the enormity of suffering in hell, some thought that Mt. Etna or other volcanoes were actually the mouth of hell. The dead, guilty of a sin they did not commit, apparently acquired infinite and eternal combustibility by dying in their "sin."

Purgatory was invented later to take the "eternity" sting out of the postmortem punishment, but that was no cakewalk either since some thought Mt. Etna was also the entrance into Purgatory. Limbo, where unbaptized infants could find some refuge had not yet been invented.

Obviously, a creator god with such a sociopathic program would not inspire warm devotion among the faithful. He would instead inspire a need to escape to gentler divine beings. And so it came to pass. That leads us to:

Third, the quest for better gods. This is where the saints came marching in, and leading their retinue was Mary, Jesus' mother. Peter Damian, in the eleventh century, spoke of her godliness, calling her *deificata*. In a hymn composed around 826 CE, Jesus addresses his mother as "most holy mother, you who have supreme command over earth and heaven." (Later theologians exerted themselves conjuring titles for her, many of which verged on divinity: mediatrix of all graces, co-redemptress, *complementum sanctissimae Trinitatis*—the latter sounding like the trinity was verging on quaternity if it needed completion by Mary.) Bernard of Clairvaux suggests that if you fear the Father, you go to Jesus, and if you fear him, you go to his mother.[20] For all practical purposes, the goddess Isis was back.

The people wanted divinities they could trust and the god they were offered did not pass muster on that count. Neither, eventually, did Jesus by his too close association with the sadistic Father God who created fallible people and then roasted them in an eternal holocaust with no hope of pardon or reprieve. Relief was needed from this terrifying situation. Mary stepped in as the *mater misericordiae*, the mother of mercy. As Jonathan Sumption said, "She offered an escape from the rigorous teaching of the church on the subject of damnation and punishment."[21] Mary even helped rogues. She was, in a word, relief from the wrath of God. That is why there are more statues of Mary in the Catholic world than of Jesus. And that is also why in reported visions and visitations (Lourdes, Fatima, Guadalupe), it is Mary, not Jesus, who regularly appears.

In all of this, we see divinity created in response to need. We also see one god (Mary) replacing another, as regularly happened in the history of the gods.

Along with Mary, the saints became the go-to beings whose status also rose to divine heights. The influential Greek theologian John of Damascus claimed that the saints were "genuinely Gods" (*alethos theoi*) and were as such proper objects of worship.[22] "The saints were the real savior-gods to whom you brought your needs and troubles," writes Dennis Nineham.[23] Relics of the saints became central to worship in this period leading one scholar to say, "the true religion of the middle ages, to be frank, is the worship of relics."[24] Relics were fought over. They had sacramental status. They were to be found everywhere from altar stones to the handles of swords. The custom of every child being given a saint's name reflects this same faith. Being buried near a saint gave hopes of resurrection. Divinity spreads.

So, the invisible realm that envelops us was more densely populated than our visible setting. Along with saints, it was also peopled by devils and angels, supernatural beings who were active in human lives. Natural events were often explained as resulting from these invisible actors. The visible world was in the grip of an invisible world not all of whose denizens were friendly. Modern Catholicism still has a rite of exorcism to banish devils who manage to control a person's body and mind. Myths die slowly. Friendly "guardian angels" began to appear around the eighth century, and were understandably welcomed.

One thing is clear: it would be inaccurate to say that the Christian religion of this period is the Christian religion of today, though echoes of its punitive spirit still haunt the experience of guilt. What is also clear is that Christianity, like all social phenomena, is a mutant. There was a long Christian tradition saying it was not changing, that Christianity was a firm and solid body of beliefs that could be handed down like family jewels. The ruling axiom was: *Nihil innovetur nisi quod traditum est*, let nothing be innovated beyond that which has been handed down. But what was handed down in the Bible, for example, was that nothing is immutable, not even "God."

It is enough to make modern seculars blush, but the ancient penchant for divinizing our achievements is still in our active repertoire. Buddhist philosopher David R. Loy writes that the traditional religions are being shunted aside by the new realities of market capitalism, which is now issuing the Shalt's and Shalt-nots to our evolving culture. It is rewriting the script on what is sacred and what is not. The Market is our shepherd, we shall not want. Unbridled freedom and consumption untethered from the rest of nature and the common good have sacramental standing.

The major religions, though not quite "moribund," are not competing well, and are not looked to as serving "a significant role in solving the environmental crisis. Their more immediate problem is whether they, like the rain forests we anxiously monitor, will survive in any recognizable form the onslaught of this new religion." "The Market," Loy argues, "is becoming the first truly world religion, binding all corners of the globe into a worldview and set of values whose religious role we overlook only because we insist on seeing them as 'secular.'"[25]

Once again, Thales is proved right: everything is indeed full of gods. We are compulsive divinizers.

Proliferation and the Christian Gods

In the history of gods, we see gods as metaphors for existing realities, not entities in themselves. These deities were the symbol of, or metaphor for, basic human needs, and also for the identity of the particular society. That practice did not end in antiquity.

As Buddhism stresses more than any other religion, framing one's identity is the basal problem confronting human personality and human collectivities. Indeed, Indian scholar Ignatius Jesudasan, a Jesuit, goes so far as to say that "religion is the metaphor or sacred mask of a secular ethical identity." His book title puts it boldly: *Religion as Metaphor for Ethno-Ethical Identity.* The point is well taken and it explains the fervor of interethnic, interracial, and inter-religious tensions that still viciously roil the human race.

Sacralized nationalized identity formation that does not include the whole human race is divisive and an incitement to violence. No heed is to be paid to humanity, said Calvin, when the honor of God is at stake. And the "honor of God" really meant the honor of one's group and personal identity. It is for this reason that denial of "God" stirs the killer instinct and leads to violence.

Good God, Bad Dualism

The metaphoric nature of god-talk shows again in what is called *dualism* in religious studies, the belief in both a good god and a god-awful one. There is a certain logic here: since we or our nations are not sinless, a second metaphor is needed to reflect the nether side. The Persian religion Zoroastrianism did this explicitly. Christianity didn't quite deify the devil but an active principle of evil that rascal certainly was. Since our identities are complex, so, too, our metaphoric gods must be.

CHAPTER 4

THE BEGINNING THAT WASN'T

The Hebrew Bible's first mistake is the opening words of its creation story, "In the beginning . . ." The Christian Bible has a creation story and it, too, has "beginning" talk: "In the beginning was the Word. . . ." Insistence on a beginning stems from limits in our imaginative powers, stunning as those vaulting powers are. Indeed, the sky would seem to be the limit in our imaginative reach, but it's not. Our imagination can only stretch so far and then it falls to its knees. And this incapacity is a factor in the formation of some religious dogmatizing. A better creation story would be that of Karen Armstrong: "In the beginning, human beings created a God who was the First Cause of all things and Ruler of heaven and earth."[1] Armstrong's "in the beginning" refers to a certain point in history where humans created the idea of a creator god.

Two stop signs that flummox our imagination are *infinity* and *nothingness*. They are beyond our imaginative grasp, and dogmas sprout at their impasse. From our *infinity* problem comes the dogma of *creatio ex nihilo* since in our experience whatever "is" had a beginning. (Actually Genesis does not say there was nothing before God's creative intervention that gave it form. God shaped the shapeless stuff that was already there.) We are best at imagining stops and starts, beginnings and endings. And so, "In the beginning." The idea of a universe that never ever did *not* exist is, in strict terms, unimaginable. It can be asserted, but not imagined. Woody Allen gave that cognitive weakness of ours a comical twist when he said, "eternity is a really long time, especially toward the end."

And from our *nothingness* problem comes the belief that the dead don't really die. They just relocate. We shrink from believing that this person who was speaking to us earlier today is now nothing except disintegrating bodily remains. The personality is gone; it is no more. Echoes of the personality linger in memory but like statues of the deceased they are not the personality that was and is no more. *Nothing* has succeeded *someone* and we cannot bear that or imagine it. And from that cognitional limit, comes the persistent, globe-spanning, counterintuitive belief that continued living is the sequel to death.

Back to the Agnostic Theists

We can *conceptualize* with our abstractive powers that which we cannot *imagine*, and so we can postulate infinity as a meaningful category in mathematics; we even create a symbol for it. When we run into the infinity-of-eternity problem, a creator God is our *deus ex machina*. In what amounts to a mind-game, we deny eternity to the universe and assign it to an X-factor that we then call "God." If we then move on to declare this X-factor "unknowable" and "incomprehensible," we have escaped the mental challenge of infinity and eternity. By assigning eternity to "God" we have relieved ourselves from the daunting idea that there is no beginning and no end to the reality of which we are a fleeting part. It is not a clean getaway since we go on to postulate a god who had no beginning.

God is such a useful hypothesis that he can do double duty. He also answers the question, *how did it happen?* How to account for the extraordinary coordination and complexity we see in marvels ranging from the fruit fly to our brains? Just say, "X did it." Of course, that is code for "we have no idea." It is really an act of despair, a kind of theistic agnosticism. *Homo primitivus* used gods to cover all gaps in our knowing. All wonders of life were attributed to the gods' agency. If a flower bloomed, it was a god who made it happen. But now that we know of plant hormones and phototropism, divine commands are not needed to let the flower do its thing. Science has closed the knowledge gap and the need for divine interventions disappears. Science has been closing gaps for the past five hundred years. Using God to avoid science's ongoing effort to trace out the little steps of evolution is the last gasp of "the God of the Gaps." We don't know how evolution happened so we will say divine intervention did it. We are then in the party of those who used to say that the rain fell and the flower bloomed because a god stepped in and made it happen.

Elan Vital

One thing that theists and nontheists all agree on is the *elan vital*, the life force that exists in the universe. It is an amazing force, incessant and unfolding. We are so impressed with this force that when we look for life on Mars or elsewhere, we only ask if the conditions for life are present. Edward O. Wilson says, "Wherever there is liquid water, organic molecules, and an energy source, there is life."[2] If those conditions are or were there, then we assume life is or was. It is assumed by many scholars that life, even intelligent life, is a "cosmic commonplace."[3] Theists can say the creator installed this life force; nontheists can simply take it as a wondrous fact of reality without positing an invisible personal designer. But when you adopt the designer hypothesis, you slide into "In the beginning" talk. You have imagined a starting point from nothing to something and you need a starter. But you also pick up some nasty problems, like how to justify the frequent tragedies the creator created.

This adaptive life force has some stunning successes—our eye is a case at point—and it also has whoppers of failures—Ebola viruses, earthquakes, tsunamis, childhood cancer, and mosquitoes, to note just a few examples. Charles Darwin, a great lover of nature, cited what he called the clumsy, wasteful, blundering, and horridly cruel works of nature. Also, and this is the ultimate downer, the life that the life force creates dies. Life is mortal both in individual cases of plants and animals and in cosmic terms like the Red Star disintegration that awaits our own beloved earth. As Carl Sagan put it, in five or six billion years the sun will become "a red giant star and will engulf the orbits of Mercury and Venus and probably the Earth. The Earth then would be inside the Sun." At that time, he wryly notes, the problems that consume us now will "appear, by comparison, modest."[4] Earth life faces earth death, a design flaw if ever there was one. Looking at the built-in tragedies of nature, Woody Allen commented that the intelligent designer is an "underachiever." That criticism might be too gentle.

Defending God

For theists, the downers produced by the life force require a "theodicy" (literally a justification of god), to justify evil in a world where god has been pictured as the benevolent *pantokrator*, omnipotent and all merciful, who holds "the whole world in his hands." Theodicy has its work cut out for it. It must find ways of seeing the tragedies knit into life as "blessings in disguise"—not easy to do when tsunamis swamp and drown men, women, children, and animals. As a last resort, theodicy declares them "mysteries," a word that dispenses from further inquiry. Natural selection does not require a theodicy. It does not have to cope with the hypothesis of an intelligent and all merciful creator-person who obviously screws up and at times seems downright sadistic.

As with god-talk, creation stories have an explanatory role; they are mythic efforts to explain life and why it is the way it is.[5] In one African creation story, the principal god sends a subordinate god to create the earth, giving him some basic elements. On the way to perform his mission he encounters other gods who are partying and drinking palm wine. They ask him to join them and he does and he overindulges. While he is in a drunken stupor another god takes the basic elements and goes off to create the world. A battle ensues when the hungover god awakes. Things did not go according to plan. Other gods—bad gods and good gods—got in on the creation project. Creation was botched. Bad things were sown along with good things and that seems to better explain the way the world is than does the Genesis story, which sees everything as "very good." Life is not all good, much less "very good." The African myth, in its simplicity, deals with that.[6]

In all god stories, the gods are a mixed bag and we are made in their image. In studying about gods, we are getting into the poetry of other peoples in other times, people who also put their minds to the conundrums of human life. Gods are the poetic art of a community. Primitive communities often grasped aspects of reality better than later literate sophisticates. It is arrogant and dumb to bypass their poetic efforts.

Back to the Nonbeginning

Those who see natural selection at work also run into mysteries as well as the cruelties and anomalies of nature. They don't pretend to be omniscient, but see the anomalies as challenges, as pointers to possible new discoveries. And they accept the reality of unanswerable questions, at least not answerable yet. Theists tend to see the mysteries of nature as a pious dispensation from further questioning, or as proof that the intelligent designer is smarter than we are so we must let it go at that. Faith in that designer gives a holiday from further questioning.

Stephen Hawking, that indefatigable and undefeatable searcher for truth, sums it up in the conclusion of his *A Brief History of Time*:

> So long as the universe had a beginning, we could suppose it has a creator. But if the universe is really completely self-contained, having no boundary or edge, it would have neither beginning nor end; it would simply be. What place then, for a creator?[7]

Pope Pius XII, speaking in 1951 to the Pontifical Academy of Sciences, opted for the creator hypothesis to which Hawking refers. He asserted: "Creation took place in time, therefore there is a Creator, therefore God exists."[8] The pope left out the big "If," that is, "If" creation took place in time. As Victor Stenger observes: "The astronomer/priest Georges-Henri Lemaitre, who first proposed the idea of a big bang, wisely advised the pope not to label this statement 'infallible.'"[9] Father Lemaitre was wise. He was in company with many prominent physicists and cosmologists who hold that the universe "has no beginning or end in space or time" but that it can be seen as having "tunneled" through the chaos "from a prior universe that existed for all previous time."[10] As Carl Sagan puts it, science sees "a universe with no edge in space, no beginning or end in time, and nothing for a Creator to do."[11]

To assert that "God" stepped into pure nothingness bringing the universe into being with a creative stroke is a hypothesis that is beyond all proving. No scientist could claim to know exactly how the universe "tunneled" into this form, but there is strong scientific support for saying that it was from something, not *ex nihilo*. Therefore, if the pope is correct that it all depends on creation in time, then the pope is wrong in his "God" conclusion. If the existence of the deity depends on creation from nothing, which is unprovable, then the pope's "God" argument is butting its head against the emerging plausibilities coming from science. The pope has "God" walking the plank of an unprovable hypothesis.

In sum, *as the pope posed the question*, the existence of "God" is unprovable. It can be urged. It can be believed. It cannot be proved.

Chance versus Intelligent Design: And the Winner Is?

The most esteemed argument for the existence of a designer-God is the "argument from order and design in the universe." It convinced me for years and I taught it as a priest-professor. It deserves to be taken seriously.

Thomas Aquinas filed the classical brief for the existence of a god at the start of his massive compendium of theology, his *Summa Theologiae*.[12] He offers "five ways" to answer in the affirmative his question *Utrum Deus Sit*, whether god is. The fifth was the argument from design and the need for a designer. The other four are a little lubricious, to put it mildly, and never had the same cachet.

The first three ways all assume the impossibility of infinity and the necessity of a beginning. They also have a sort of sleight-of-hand quality to them. Briefly, the first proof is based on motion. All things are potentially in motion but to move from being potentially in motion to being actually in motion requires an outside mover. This cannot go back *in infinitum*, Thomas insists, so there must have been an unmoved mover way back there to get all motion started. And the unmoved mover, he says, is what "all understand to be God."

The second argument is similar but based on the need for effects to have causes. But the string of causes cannot stretch back into infinity, Thomas states, and therefore there had to be a first uncaused cause, and "all name this cause God." The third argument is sibling to the other two: things we know have the possibility of being or not being. Things move from being possible to being actual *ex aliunde*, from some outside cause. They cannot do it themselves. If everything is potentially not in being, we would end up with nothing. Therefore there must be a being that necessarily is and has no possibility of not being, and that being Thomas says "*omnes dicunt Deum*."

The fourth proof is the most slippery. It takes specious to an abysmal level. It is based, Thomas says, on the fact that realities like truth and goodness exist in *more or less* forms. This means that there must be a peak, a maximum, underlying all lesser manifestations, and we call this maximum God, *dicimus Deum*. That is a bridge too far. Richard Dawkins gives it the *reductio ad absurdum* treatment. People vary in smelliness, so there must be a "preeminently peerless stinker" out there somewhere and that maximum of smelliness would be "God."[13]

Thomas's fifth argument is the one that spans the history of god-talk and is the prime argument in our day. Things that lack knowledge, says Thomas, act purposefully. This can't be by chance. The well-directed arrow points to an intelligent archer and, likewise, those complex things in nature that work so well and so consistently are guided by the unseen designer we call "God."

This old argument appears today in more sophisticated dress and no one has taken it on as earnestly or as well as Richard Dawkins. Among the current coterie of popular atheists, Dawkins is not panicked by the god hypothesis. Wit is always there, winking at the brim of his writing. He is an atheist missionary who admits that conversion is his goal.[14] But he does not follow Sam Harris over the edge. Harris's faith-phobia—"Our enemy is nothing other than faith itself"—festers into a rabid Islamophobia that makes the bloody Christian Crusaders look half-hearted. Harris says breathlessly that if an "Islamic regime" gets nuclear weaponry, "the only thing likely to ensure our survival may be a nuclear first strike of our own." This "would kill tens of millions of innocent civilians in a single day—but it may be the only course of action available to us, given what Islamists believe."[15] We must "win the war" against this Islamic menace, or "bondage" will be our fate.[16] (Down boy!)

No, Dawkins is not out to nuke believers; he just wants to argue against them with his gifted pen. Dawkins also proves that atheism is not inimical to a warm sense of humor. Indeed all those in this conversation should heed the wisdom of G. K. Chesterton: "Life is serious all the time, but living cannot be. You may have all the solemnity you wish in your neckties, but in anything important (such as sex, death, and religion), you must have mirth or you will have madness."[17] Chesterton might not agree with Dawkins but he could sit and have a drink with him.

Chance or Designer, the False Dichotomy

The argument from design, Thomas Aquinas's fifth and only argument deserving a hearing, stands or falls on the *chance v. design* dichotomy. A monkey (representing chance) plucking at a typewriter for an infinite amount of time will not produce the likes of a Shakespearean play or a poetic saga like the *Aeneid*. Only an intelligent designer will do that. A hurricane (chance) blowing through a scrap yard will not assemble a Boeing 747 or a Honda minivan even if the hurricane lasted a million years. *Voila!* Moving in for the kill, the designer-ists say the wonders of nature, more complex than planes, automobiles, or literary classics demand a designer, too. Chance, even if we could define it, is not up to the challenge. And, because chance cannot explain all the wonders of nature, the referee raises the arm of intelligent design as the winner and still champion.

Chance, matched up against intelligent design, should have pleaded *nolo contendere* before the fight started. Chance, in that false dichotomy, is a straw man waiting to be pummeled and dismissed to make way for "God."

Chance will never explain the complexity of nature, a complexity so great that the naked eye cannot even see most of its intricacies. Let's go really microscopic and start with a cell. "Measured in bits of pure information, the genome of a cell is comparable to all editions of the *Encyclopedia Britannica* published since its inception in 1768. . . . If the DNA helices in one cell of a mouse, a typical animal species, were placed end on end and magically enlarged to have the same width as wrapping string, they would extend for over nine hundred kilometers, with about four thousand nucleotide pairs packed into every meter."[18] Chance could not coordinate all of that. On that we can all agree.

So we have found common ground with the purveyors of "intelligent design." Chance is not the answer and no scientist thinks it is. *Chance v. intelligent design* is a fake fight. *Intelligent designer v. natural selection*, that is the real fight.

Now it must be admitted at first blush that there are many things in nature that seem to cry out for a personal designer. Modern designer-ists are rushing into biology to put examples of such on the table. They look for examples of "irreducible complexity," that is, a natural construction so complex that the removal of even one part of it causes the whole to stop functioning. Design-ists offer the Venus' Flower Basket where millions of microscopic cells conspire to produce a million glassy splinters and build them into an intricate and effective lattice. Chance could not do that, say the designer-ists. And natural selection scientists like Richard Dawkins agree wholeheartedly. The utter statistical improbability of that phenomenon being the product of chance is not just implausible, it's silly. Says Dawkins: "The greater the statistical improbability, the less plausible is chance as a solution: that is what improbable means."[19]

Accusing those who reject the theistic hypothesis of enshrining chance as the explanation of everything on the evolutionary slope is false and self-serving.

The Alternative to Chance

Natural selection tries to explain—often successfully and factually—what chance could never explain. Natural selection is the alternative to a personalized super being who started and runs the universe, handling everything from star formation to the Venus' Flower Basket.

Like Jesus, Richard Dawkins likes to teach with parables, like the very helpful *Climbing Mount Improbable.* But first, let us go back to our humble biological origins. Charles Birch and John Cobb highlight the marvel of life's beginning:

> The evolution of a living cell from organic molecules may have happened more than once on the earth. But probably only one original cell gave rise to all the rest of life on earth. This seems to be the only possible explanation of the basic similarity of the cells of all living organisms. All use the same DNA code and similar amino acids. The doctrine of evolution holds that from one beginning all the diversity of life on earth, its two billions of species (of which two million known species are alive today) and the many varieties within those species, have arisen. Life is like a great branching tree with one central stem.[20]

We have come a long way from *the little cell that could.* All kinds of improbable things happened on the way as life unfolded, ranging from wonders like eyes, honey bees, eagle's wings, and a baby's first smile. Humanity stands at the foot of Mount Improbable, facing the mystery of how we went from such simplicity to such coordinated and often beautiful complexity. Take the human eye and put it on top of Mount Improbable. Charles Darwin said that saying natural selection produced the eye's inimitable contrivances for adjusting focus to different distances and for admitting just the right amount of light sounds absurd. It is absurd if you take the short view; it is not if you study the steps of evolutionary process as Darwin first taught us to do.

One side of Dawkins' Mount Improbable is a sheer cliff, impossible to climb; but the other side is a long, very long gentle slope moving to the summits. "The absurd notion that such complexities could spontaneously self-assemble is symbolized by leaping from the foot of the cliff to the top in one bound."[21] Evolution does not do that. Natural selection and evolutionary science go around to the back of the mountain and creep and crawl in itsy-bitsy steps up the gentle slope to the summit, finding clues for some things along the way. There is wisdom in this because a lot of evidence of small adaptations await the patient climber on the long slope. Darwin discovered, and subsequent studies confirm, that complex organs are formed by numerous successive, slight modifications, as new forms and species take shape. In many cases, the fossil evidence shows some of the steps. As Dawkins says: "Many evolutionary transitions are elegantly documented by more or less continuous series of gradually changing intermediate fossils. Some are not, these are the famous 'gaps.'"[22]

However, the reason why evolution and natural selection are not "just a theory" is that the record is not all "gaps." A lot of the mutations and adaptations are there and, as Dawkins says, "elegantly documented." This is a theory well grounded in solid discoveries. There is exciting evidence about how life moved out of the seas and developed new ways of getting oxygen. But, actually, we do not have to go further than the museum of our own bodies to see evidence of the adaptive evolutionary process.

Carl Sagan asks: "Why do we have ten fingers? Because we evolved from a Devonian fish that has ten phalanges in its fins. If we evolved from a Devonian fish that had twelve phalanges, we would be counting things on our twelve fingers. Then ten would lose its hegemonic post."[23] (We might have decided that it takes twelve yards to make a first down.) Expanding on our fishy start, Neil Shubin, in his book *Your Inner Fish*, notes that our inner ear is "modified fish-head architecture" just as our limbs are modified fins. Fish were not designed to walk; no wonder we have knee problems.[24] As Larry L. Rasmussen says, "it literally takes a universe to raise a child . . . the scaffolding for our entire body was already present in those most ancient of creatures, single-celled animals, the ones from which all life evolved."[25]

We have toes as a result of our ancestors' life in the high forests, our forebears swinging from branch to branch. We don't need toes much now. The big one is good for balance, but the rest of them are easily stubbable relics of evolution, like the vermiform appendix that is on its way out. We see in our bodies the process of an evolution that is still ongoing at its own infinitesimal pace. When our sun dies in some six billion years, astrophysicist Martin Rees says that any intelligent creatures witnessing the phenomenon will be entities as different from us as we are from a bug—and that comparison may understate it. When we do think of "extraterrestrials," we think of them as being like us although with different shaped heads and organs. Such thinking is too parochial to fit in the universe of infinite variables.

Human hubris could not swallow Copernicus' dismissal of our centrality. We tend to think of ourselves as the peak and pinnacle of nature's genius. We may actually be a retarded species, technological adolescents in comparison with other intelligent beings in the infinite expanse of the cosmos. It is not kooky to think of such. Harvard University and the Planetary Society, a 100,000-member worldwide organization, have embarked on a sophisticated search for extraterritorial intelligence. There may be intelligent beings thousands or millions of years more advanced than our "civilization."[26] Ongoing Copernican rethink is a major unmet need.

There are many phenomena in nature where fossil evidence is not there and so tracing the myriad intermediate steps is impossible, but the principle of adaptation is amply witnessed by what we do know. All this accumulating data favors the slope of evolution rather than the imaginary leap up to an intelligent designer. We should invite the theistic intelligent designer-ists over to the long sloping side of Mount Improbable where they could help us answer some of the questions of how evolution unfolded. Their time would be better spent on that side of the mountain.

God and Billiards

In the face of complexity, the theist goes agnostic and postulates an invisible maker. Don't look for steps along the way; just say X did it and then call X "God." However, there are theists who admit to the fact of evolution. That is welcome and not surprising since evolution is a theory only in the sense that there is no other plausible theory. Evolutionary theists argue that the tortuous climb up the evolutionary slope is the unfolding of the master plan of the intelligent designer. As a skilled billiards player hits one ball setting all the others in motion in the way the player wished, so God gave the evolutionary process the initial tilt and the map it must follow. This way evolutionary theists have God and evolution, too, and every discovery made is a discovery of the master plan the designer-god instilled in the process at its inception.

Even Charles Darwin, in his *On the Origin of Species*, got pressed into this view. In the first edition of the book, this was his last sentence: "There is grandeur in this view of life, with its several powers, having been originally breathed into a few forms or into one; and that, whilst this planet has gone cycling on according to the fixed law of gravity, from so simple a beginning endless forms most beautiful and most wonderful have been, and are being, evolved." In the sixth edition of the book, however, after his book had elicited a storm of criticism from theists, he gave a nod to "God." Referring to the powers that drive evolution, he added that these powers were "breathed by the Creator into a few forms, etc." But this theistic add-on changed nothing and added nothing to the eloquent panegyric he composed about the wonders and beauties that emerged from the swirl of evolution.

Darwin did not let himself get pushed into theodicy to justify the bad stuff that this Creator breathed into the evolutionary process. Recall that Darwin was a realist regarding the "clumsy, wasteful, blundering and horridly cruel works of nature." He left theodicy, that irremediable embarrassment, to the theists.

Theoretically, this form of billiard theism could also allow for an eternal material reality with a god calling the shots as our universe "tunneled" out of a previous universe. But there is one problem this designer-god *cum* evolution does not escape. The more science tells us about the world, the more the designer has to answer for. The theist who minored in theodicy now must major in it. If the Grand Designer made a universe where life springs up whenever the basics are there, and if intelligent life is "a cosmic commonplace," and if the number of galaxies beyond the Milky Way may number in the hundreds of thousands of millions, divinity would first of all seem understaffed if only one god had all of this in his portfolio. But worse yet—and here is where sadism enters the picture—explosions are the norm, from supernovas to quasars. As Carl Sagan says, "obliterations of whole planets" are a regular occurrence, obliteration that is built into the system, obliteration of any life, intelligent or not, that had developed there.[27] This paints a horrible picture of the "Prime Cause" or "Prime Mover" who would make life possible and then plan its obliteration and a brutal return to chaos as a matter of course. Theism promises simplicity and security and delivers neither. It is a troubled hypothesis that creates problems it cannot solve. But it is a seductive hypothesis that consolingly smothers all the unanswered questions of evolution with a buoyant and evasive "God did it" reply.

PART II

THE DIVINITY OF JESUS

CHAPTER 5

THE GREATEST STORY NEVER TOLD

The Ascent to Godhood

Jesus had a long and tortuous path to divinity, getting more than a little boost early on from a Roman Emperor—a striking irony since it was that same Roman Empire that murdered him. As Robert W. Funk puts it: "Jesus was gradually elevated to godhood in the second and third centuries. But Christianity took its definitive form—the form defined by the emperor and the church councils as 'orthodox'—in the fourth century with the creation of the first creeds and canons."[1]

Jesus would never be able to understand Christology. Jesus is described in Mark's gospel, the oldest of the gospels, as part of a large family. He had four brothers, James, Joseph, Judas, and Simon. He also had several sisters, whose names we are not given but who were well known and spoken of in the town of Nazareth, a hamlet of some 300 residents (Mark 6:1–6).

Once Upon a Time

Here are some things that could never have happened in the Jewish world of Jesus.

He could never have sat down at dinner one evening with his Jewish brothers and sisters, and explained to them that he, unlike the rest of the family, had preexisted eternally before his birth as the Second Person of a Holy Trinity—and that all three divine persons combined to make only one divinity, one god. If he made this announcement, his siblings would have to be excused if they began to think that their brother had overindulged in wine or had gone totally mad.

If Jesus, with his foreknowledge, went on to tell his siblings that he would be crucified by the Romans, it might not be surprising to them since Galilee was a trouble zone for the Romans and the crucifixion of Galilean rebels was not uncommon. However, it would shock his family to hear that his crucifixion, unlike all the others, would not be due to his resistance to the Roman occupation, but would be a preplanned human/divine sacrifice to atone for the sins of all the people who ever existed or whoever would exist. The family knew about animal sacrifice in the temple, but a return to primitive human sacrifice with their brother as the victim would have been abhorrent. If Jesus, dipping further into his divine foreknowledge, said that for centuries thereafter cathedrals would be built all over the world to celebrate this brutal human sacrifice as the central liturgy of the religion founded on their brother, their jaws would have dropped even further.

If he pressed on with his story, he could have told them that in the great cathedrals of the future a ritual would be performed, which would involve eating his body and drinking his blood under the form of bread and wine and that his living body, disguised as unleavened bread, would be stored in golden tabernacles, with a votive light lit before it to signal his real presence.

None of this tall tale would have squared with their experience of their brother. Jesus, after all, was no ascetic. He seems to have been more of a "hail fellow well met." He was criticized for feasting and partying while John the Baptist fasted (Mark 2:18–19). Clearly their brother was a bit of a party animal. He was a regular at dinner parties. As Bible scholar and Dominican priest Albert Nolan says: "These dinner parties were such a common feature of Jesus' life that he could be accused of being a drunkard and a glutton."[2] Joseph A. Grassi writes: "Unlike the Baptist, Jesus drank wine and alcohol at the homes and 'taverns' of the day."[3] Clearly their cousin John the Baptist would have been a better candidate for godliness, except that claiming godliness was so un-Jewish.

If his family were still listening and not yet bowled over with laughter, Jesus might then let them in on the news that, bad as his forthcoming death would be, he would be back in three days fit as a fiddle. (This would be particularly galling to his brother James who was also executed as a rebel with no promise of a mere triduum in the grave.)

Moving on, Jesus might deliver the real shocker of the evening, breaking the news to his siblings that their dad, Joseph, was not his dad even though their mother Mary was his mother. Startling news like that could strain family ties. It would certainly raise questions, like "If our dad Joseph is not your father, who is?" Jesus then would explain that the Holy Spirit had "overshadowed" their mother, as two of the Gospels to be written a generation later would put it, and she conceived without benefit of sexual intercourse. By way of further explanation he would remind them that the Holy Spirit who had caused the impregnation is the third person of the triune God of which he, their brother, was the second.

This could only raise further wildly troubling questions. If the Holy Spirit got their mother pregnant, and if Jesus and the Holy Spirit were one God, then it would follow that Jesus was his own father. This would seriously complicate Jesus' relationships with his mother and might even elicit nasty epithets from his incredulous siblings. Jesus, to be honest, would have to admit that this unusual impregnation almost caused a split between their mom and dad. When Joseph found that Mary was "with child by the Holy Spirit" before Joseph himself had had sex with her, he thought it a bit of a tall tale and was minded to put an end to the relationship. It took an apparition of an angel—angelic apparitions are hard to come by when you have a surprise pregnancy to explain—to convince him that the Holy Spirit truly was the third party in this holy ménage à trois (Matt. 1:18–25; Luke 1:26–38). Also, if Jesus and his divine Father were of "one and the same being," he in another sense was his own father. It really would become staggeringly convoluted.

Jesus with his foreknowledge would have to admit that his story of Incarnation would prove a hard sell down through the years. Inquiring minds would want to know why only one person of the Trinity got to do the incarnation thing. To provide balance and stay charges of sexism in the Godhead, the Father or the Spirit could have incarnated as a woman. St. Anselm, an eleventh-century intellectual, pondered these possible incarnational permutations. He put it this way: "If the Father were to take flesh, there would be two grandsons in the Trinity, since by becoming a man, he would be the grandson of Mary's parents, and the Word, without taking on humanity in any way would be the Son of her son. All such possibilities are unfitting and do not occur if it is the Word who becomes man."[4] *If the Father were the son of Mary, he would be his own grandson. Ten centuries after Anselm, Garry Wills allowed that all this speculation might remind irreverent people of the 1947 Latham-Jaffe song, "I'm My Own Grandpa."*[5]

Only Matthew and Luke told the virgin birth story. Mark, John, and Paul gave it a pass. Maybe they thought it indelicate to go there. After all, there was a disquieting rumor circulating of Jesus' illegitimate birth that would cast a dark shadow on the gospel story. In her book, "The Illegitimacy of Jesus," Bible scholar Jane Schaberg argues that the tradition of "an illegitimate conception" preceded the story of "a miraculous virginal conception," the latter being, as Joseph had suspected, a strained coverup.[6]

And so ends the story that Jesus never told.

The Perils of Anachronism

Virginal conception and other OB/GYN issues aside, it would be a mortal sin of anachronism to take the christological ideas that were formed laboriously, imaginatively, and contentiously by Christians in subsequent centuries—using Greek idioms—and interject them into the Jewish home of Joseph and Mary, the couple Luke's gospel refers to simply as Jesus' "parents" (Luke 2:33). Such claims of triune and incarnate gods would not have made any sense and would indeed have seemed blasphemous to Jewish ears. Jesus' family (and neighbors) had trouble even accepting Jesus' more modest claim to be a prophetic rabbi with a mission to serve the *regnum Dei* on earth as other prophets had done. John's Gospel says: "his brothers had no faith in him" (John 7:5). (Maybe if he showed them he could walk on water, he might have convinced them.)

Which Jesus?

In seeking the "essence" of the Christian religion, Catholic theologian Hans Kung has a simple answer. Christianity is based on the "all-determining significance of a concrete human figure, Jesus the Christ."[7] Jesus is "the golden thread" that holds twenty centuries of

Christianity together.[8] If only that were true, it would be so convenient. The problem is there is no one Jesus or one thread in the Bible or in subsequent Christian history. Kung's tidy solution runs smack into the "which Jesus?" problem.

The Jesus mitosis starts in the gospels. Which Jesus do you choose? The one who is "meek and humble of heart" with nowhere to rest his head, or the not-so-meek or humble Jesus of the great "I am" texts? "I am the way and the truth and the life. . . . I and the Father are one and no one but no one comes to the Father except through me." Is it the Jesus of the Ebionites and Arians, who just might have been closer to what Jesus thought of himself? Or is it the Jesus defined (or spun) at the Nicaean council housed in Constantine's summer home, a suspicious birthplace for high Christology? Is it the love-your-enemies and turn-the-other-cheek Jesus or the vengeful, truculent Jesus of the Book of Revelation whose "eyes flamed like fire," was armed with a "sharp sword" and wore "a garment drenched in Blood" (19:11–15)? The multiplication of Christs was well on its way before the biblical canon closed.

Reflecting mature biblical sophistication, Walter Brueggemann writes that David was "the dominant figure in Israel's narrative." Yet he disclaims interest in the "historical David" who, Brueggemann says, "is not available to us." What we have is the "constructed David," and we must settle for that. "What is important is that David is the engine for Israel's imagination. . . . This David is no doubt a literary, imaginative construction, made by many hands. . . . We cannot get behind the literary construction, even as we cannot get behind the construction of any significant person."[9]

For "David" in those sentences, substitute "Jesus." We have a literary construction—nay, multiple literary constructions of Jesus, and our role is to look for the moral gold that lies there, wrapped in swaddling myths but still allowing us to respond positively to the question from John's gospel: "Can anything good come out of Nazareth?" (John 1:46). In spite of the literary and imaginative barriers that stand between us and the Jesus of history, the quest to penetrate the constructions still lures scholars. Increased knowledge of the culture in which he lived fuels suppositions of what the real Jesus was like. The search for echoes from his actual life, however faint, is a continuing lure.

Christian faith insists that Jesus was fully human. Bible scholar William E. Phipps writes: "Along with all the orthodox Christians I believe that Jesus was fully human and I think that sexual desire is intrinsic to human nature."[10] No one can know for sure if Jesus was heterosexual, homosexual, or bisexual in his orientation. The only truly scholarly answer on that question is, "Who knows?" The gospels say nothing of his having children, but the gospels were not biographies. They were involved in the literary construction of Jesus and each had a missionary axe to grind. Martin Luther was cocksure that Jesus had sexual feelings and acted them out. Luther's friend, Pastor John Schlaginhaufen, recorded this remarkable comment in 1532:

> Christ was an adulterer for the first time with the woman at the well, for it was said, "nobody knows what he's doing with her" (John 4:27). Again with Magdalene, and still again with the adulterous woman in John 8, whom he let off so easily. So the good Christ had to become an adulterer before he died.[11]

This comment was in Luther's *Table Talk*, and who of us should be held responsible for comments after a good meal enhanced by heart-gladdening beverages. It seems though that Luther accepted the common belief that Jesus, for some reason, was certainly not married, and that accounts for his nonmarital sexual activity. As Phipps says: "Luther believed that the satisfaction of all physical appetites was necessary."[12] At any rate, poor Jesus endures what few of us will have to: speculation on our sex lives two millennia after our death. The dominant need for most Christians historically to believe Jesus was not married speaks volumes on our queasy attitudes toward our sexuality and our bodies.

The Docetist Escape

Early on in the Jesus movement, there was hesitancy about the possibility of blending divinity and humanity. These doubts took on the name of "docetism" (from the Greek *dokeo*, "I seem"). We see worries about it already in the Christian part of the Bible, in 1 John

4:1–3, 2 John 7, and Colossians 2:8, where there are warnings against seeing Jesus as not being truly "in the flesh." It is often assumed that docetism fell dead under the anathematizing blows of the orthodox, but that is a mistake. Docetism could be the *de facto* dominant view of the faithful today who find more comfort in John's high Christology of Jesus as preexistent "Word" and prefer it to a Jesus who ate, slept, drank wine, went fishing, and who fully experienced the grand force of eroticism. The humanity of Jesus casts a shadow on the divinity of Christ. As Robert W. Funk puts it: "The Christ of the Christian confession of faith has all but eliminated the Jesus of history."[13] This accounts for the triumph of the docetic "heresy." Robin R. Meyers puts it bluntly: "Docetism, which asserts that Jesus was not a man at all, but merely God masquerading as a man, is the dominant heresy in the church today."[14] Greek attitudes toward the body contributed to this. Again Funk: "For hellenized Christians, Jesus the iconoclast became Christ the icon."[15] And the icon had to be dis-incarnated.

It is pure speculation on my part, but that might also explain why it is Mary, not Jesus, who appears in the "apparitions" claimed by Catholics. Apparitions in the flesh would make Jesus too human, and that offends docetic tastes. Mary's body does not offend. No docetism has stripped her of her humanity. So she keeps showing up. As Leonard Shlain observes: "The Church has authenticated over twenty-one thousand sightings of Mary."[16] Against those numbers, Jesus cannot compete. Jesus' humanity stirs uneasiness still.[17]

Flaws Creep In

All the gospel authors viewed Jesus in a positive light. Therefore, when something less edifying about Jesus is mentioned, it has some *prima facie* credibility. In Mark's gospel, Jesus flunks out on ecumenism and shows that, unlike Paul, he was no "apostle to the Gentiles." The story is told of a Gentile woman, "a Phoenician of Syria." She asks for a cure from Jesus for her daughter. Jesus was not even polite. "Let the children be satisfied first; it is not fair to take the children's bread and throw it to the dogs." The woman who had just been called a dog persisted, saying: "even the dogs under the table eat the children's scraps" (Mark 7:27–28). That impressed Jesus and he granted her the favor she asked. Still it is the woman who is morally impressive here, not Jesus.

Jesus did inherit from Isaiah and his Judaism the ideal of peace-making. Yet, applying the old wisdom, "show me your friends and I'll tell you what you are," Jesus has a problem. The twelve he chose as special comrades were a mixed bag, including one named Judas Iscariot. The Zealots were a wild bunch who lived by the sword, "fighters from the cradle," as Josephus said. Even after the terrible sacking of Jerusalem in 70 CE by Titus, they kept up the guerilla warfare against the Romans for another three years. When finally surrounded, they committed mass suicide. They were, to put it clearly, men of violence, and strange company for Jesus. Yet, there was Judas Iscariot, one of the vicious *sicarii*. Josephus tells us that they operated in crowds, carrying small daggers under their garments to cut the throats of their opponents and then melt away into the crowd. Again, strange company for the Jesus of the Sunday Schools.

Then there is the story of Jesus' disorderly conduct in the temple. "He upset the tables of the money-changers and the seats of the dealers in pigeons; and he would not allow anyone to use the temple courts as a thoroughfare for carrying goods" (Mark: 11:15–16). This was not Jesus in a "turn-the-other-cheek-walk-the-extra-mile" mood. For that kind of disorderly conduct today, as Meyers says, Jesus "would be arrested as a public nuisance and ordered to take anger-management classes."[18] None of these stories make Jesus less interesting nor do they diminish the towering moral vision attributed to him, but they do clash with favored stereotypes of Jesus the Christ.

Was the Church Jesus' Idea?

Orthodoxy, especially Catholic orthodoxy, wants to believe that Jesus founded the church and gave it specific governmental structure and sacraments. Not true. Jesus was a reformer within Judaism. There is no indication he wanted to set up a competing religious organization. For one thing, many scholars, not all, think that he expected the end of this age to be coming soon, even within months according to some.[19] The last thing he needed was to start a church.[20] In fact, the Jesus movement did not even separate from the synagogue until the latter part of the first century. Again, Hans Kung, a Catholic priest and theologian: "The man from Nazareth, without any office and dignities, had proclaimed the kingdom of God, but he had not wanted to create a special community distinct from Israel with its own creed and cult, its own constitution and ministries."[21] So Jesus did not found a church or institute its sacraments, as subsequent orthodoxies would insist.

Roman or Christian?

There is an added irony and another reason to call the Roman Catholic Church *Roman*. Not only was the Roman Emperor Constantine a party to the divinization of Jesus, but Roman law also shaped the papacy. The papacy, with its claim that the pope is the "vicar of Christ," was not original equipment in the early Jesus movement that later morphed into the church. The commonly held belief that Peter the apostle was the first pope is wrong and anachronistic. The papacy took form mainly in the fifth century under the aegis of Leo I, bishop of Rome. Trained in Roman law, he simply took the titles and majestic claims developed by Emperor Augustus to enhance the office of emperor and applied them to himself in Peter's name. But Peter had nothing to do with it. As Walter Ullmann put it, Leo and others simply transferred the "characteristically Roman ideas [of imperial power] to the function of the pope and to his *auctoritas*."[22] The popes still claim the title fashioned by Augustus, "the supreme pontiff" ("pontiff" meaning, etymologically, the bridge maker between earth and heaven). The monarchical papacy that resulted from this expropriation of Roman imperial pomp is heretical to what we do know of the early Jesus story.

The Constructed Jesus

The point is that what we have in hand are literary constructions of Jesus. Jesus wrote nothing and we have no idea which of the words attributed to him are his. In fact, John Dominic Crossan says that between 95 percent and 97 percent of the Jewish state was illiterate at the time of Jesus and so "it must be presumed that Jesus also was illiterate." As in any oral culture, the foundational narratives of the culture would be known to him but he could not bandy texts in the temple with the learned scribes, as Luke would have us believe (Luke 2:41–52).[23] The "Sermon on the Mount" is seen as his masterpiece and yet it was not original. It was Jewish to the core. As Pinchas Lapide, an Orthodox Jew, says of the Sermon: "The plaster, the cement, and all the building stones come from Jewish quarries." There are hundreds of pages of rabbinic parallels and analogues to every verse in the Sermon on the Mount.[24] That makes sense since Jesus was in the train of the Exodus/Sinai epic that inspired both Judaism and Christianity. To that visionary moral narrative and its stunning contemporaneity, I will return in Part IV.

Could Anything Good Come Out of Nicaea?

Mise en scéne: At the conclusion of the Council at Nicaea, a council summoned by Constantine to get agreement on who Jesus was so that Christianity might better serve as a stable glue for his sprawling empire, a celebratory banquet was thrown. The description of this banquet by Eusebius shows how far the movement had gone from the poverty of Jesus' Nazareth. In a context of military guards with drawn swords and imperial luxury, Jesus got redefined.

> Detachments of the bodyguard and troops surrounded the entrance of the place with drawn swords, and through the midst of them the men of God proceeded without fear into the innermost of the Imperial apartments, in which some were the Emperor's companions at table, while others reclined on couches arranged on either side. One might have thought that a picture of Christ's kingdom was thus shadowed forth. (Eusebius, Life of Constantine, 3:15)

* * *

Jesus had a lot of success as a moral teacher, drawing on the rich spirituality of his Judaism and relying on the prophets of Israel, especially Isaiah. He could not, however, have earned a professorship in

Christology. (If he was illiterate, how could he get tenure?) Jesus is of little help in answering the question that has so vexed Christian theologians. Council Fathers at Nicaea and Chalcedon and subsequent councils labored hard to nail down Jesus' identity. They developed what came to be called *Christology*. It would be most consoling to the Fathers of these councils if we could show that Jesus agreed with them on their answers to the question, "Who is he?"

Sad to tell, there is no evidence that Jesus' own Christology was orthodox or at peace with later councils like Nicaea or Chalcedon or any of those that followed. Indeed, the plot thickens and confusion mounts when we look into the three hundred years following Jesus' death. Those years show that Nicaea's definition of Jesus as of "one being" with the Father was a novelty. Christology began with the honest question of those who heard Jesus. They asked, "Who is this?" (Mark 4:41; Luke 7:49, 8:25). They did not come up with the answer that he was equal to Yahweh. Jewish Christians were not about to make that leap. But it wasn't just the Jewish Christians who were out of sync with what Nicaea came up with. Hans Kung writes:

> If we wanted to judge Christians of the pre-Nicene period, in the light of the Council of Nicaea, then not only the Jewish Christians would be heretics but also almost all the Greek church fathers . . . since as a matter of course they taught a subordination of the "Son" to the "Father" which according to the later criterion of the definition of a "sameness of substance" (*homoousia*) was regarded by the Council of Nicaea as heretical. In the light of this we can hardly avoid the question: if one wants to make just the Council of Nicaea the criterion instead of the New Testament, was anyone at all orthodox in the early church of the first centuries?[25]

The "made up" quality of Christology shines brightly in Kung's candid words.

This is an astounding state of affairs. It indicates a radical break between the early churches and what was later copper fastened into an official orthodoxy. Would the real heretics stand up! Is the exuberant, if often contradictory, poetry of the early Jesus movement to be sacrificed to the metaphysical Jesus concocted in Greco-Roman philosophical terms under imperial pressure at Nicaea? And then that terribly honest question: Why? Why prefer the metaphysical Jesus to the Jesus of earlier times? Dare we match the scorn of those who questioned anything good coming out of Nazareth by asking, "Could anything good come out of Nicaea?"

Should it not be seen as disconcerting, and indeed, baffling, that all early Christians, those who were closer to Jesus and his times, were "heretical" and at odds with the solemn convoluted definitions of subsequent councils and creeds? Does this not undermine the whole field of Christology?

Hans Kung tries to face the problem and offers a solution. Go back to the New Testament. There, he implies, we will find the straight scoop on Jesus and the answer to Mark's and Luke's question: "Who is this?"

Alas, the New Testament does not even try to do what Nicaea tried to do. There is no unified answer to the "who is this" question. New Testament Christology is a hodgepodge. Jesus himself bears blame for this. He did not seem to have taken an interest in settling the question of who he was—since he probably thought who he *was* was pretty obvious, and he did not anticipate that centuries of Christians would go into contortions dreaming up ideas about who he was. He probably would have thought their time better spent concentrating on and putting into practice what he said about ending poverty and tyranny and making peace. Had he spoken clearly on who he was, his followers could not have been so confused and divided right from the start on precisely that point. As Oxford University biblical scholar Dennis Nineham says: "Jesus cannot have thought and taught about himself what later orthodoxy attributed to him. If he had, the wide variety of views about his origins, nature and work, among his devoted early followers would be quite beyond explanation."[26]

Nineham then imagines a modern field anthropologist being taken on a magic carpet back to the Mediterranean world in the second half of the first century. The anthropologist would find groups who traced their beliefs to the Jesus who preached in Palestine, was crucified at the orders of Pontius Pilate (Roman procurator of Judea from 26 to 36 CE), and was somehow still alive after all that. Beyond that central conviction, the observer would find very little unanimity. Some would insist Jesus had only been a man "raised up" by God just as God had raised up prophets and kings. Some believed Jesus was not the big event but only a messenger to prepare for a supernatural figure known as "the Son of Man" who was to come later. Others would say Jesus was a product of a mixed divine and human conception. Some would say Jesus preexisted before his earthly birth, others would not claim that. Various groups had high expectations of an imminent glorious return of Jesus, called the Parousia, and many were puzzled as to why it had not happened already. This belief was so prevalent that some of them thought it useless to get married or even carry on with their jobs.[27]

The carpet-riding anthropologist transported back to that time would be impressed by "the mythological character of all the interpretations he encountered" and the relationship of those interpretations to dominant myths in other religions in that region at that time. Poetic freedom rather than journalistic fixation on verifiable facts marked these fluid interpretations of Jesus and his life. Nicaea's passion for Greco-Roman philosophy as the best way to define Jesus was a world apart from Jesus' immediate contemporaries. They saw Jesus for what he was, a Jew understood and described in thoroughly Jewish terms, like "the Son of Man," "the Son of David," "Messiah," "Son of God," "rabbi," and "prophet." As Elaine Pagels says: "Although Mark and the other evangelists use titles that Christians today often take as indicating Jesus' divinity," when the first gospel was forming "these titles designated *human* roles. . . . Mark's contemporaries would most likely have seen Jesus as a *man*—although one gifted, as Mark says, with the power of the holy spirit, and divinely appointed to rule in the coming kingdom of God."[28] Such thinking would be excoriated at Nicaea but it was Mark's version of "Gospel truth."[29]

Bible to the Rescue?

The formation of the Christian Bible, the "New Testament" canon, was an effort to pick the winners amid the diverse writings that proliferated. It was a long process that took place over some two hundred years. All canons in literature or religion sin by mistaken inclusions and exclusions and the New Testament followed suit. Kung's hope for it as a rescue is not fulfilled. The orthodoxy of the councils stands on the high Christology that posits Jesus as the preexistent second person of the Trinity. The Bible is not friendly to that assertion. As Catholic theologian Kung concedes: "There is no trace of a real pre-existence christology, far less of a triune God in either Paul or John." There is also no assertion of preexistence in Luke or Matthew, and Matthew and Luke do not hesitate to include in their gospels "passages which show no sign of regarding Jesus as divine." In the New Testament, says Kung, "there is no doctrine of one God in three persons . . . no doctrine of a 'triune God,' a 'Trinity.'"[30] This was a later, a fourth-century construction. The Nicaean fathers would have put Kung (and me) to the stake for saying such things. But the fact is, as A. N. Wilson says, "we can discount the idea that Jesus ever claimed to be the Second Person of the Trinity, or that he ever claimed to be God, since the New Testament never states that he made any such claim. We can even discount that Jesus ever thought of himself as the pre-existent Logos."[31] E. P. Sanders says that "the Gospels show Jesus as remarkably reluctant to say who he was."[32] It wasn't his fault if it became an obsession for subsequent centuries of Christians. Jesus, the Jew who grew up in Nazareth, did not have an identity crisis. It was the Christianity that happened after him that imposed it on him.

Jesus as Christological Nuisance

When church councils undertook to redefine Jesus in their own terms, they could and did point to John's Gospel. "When all things began, the Word already was. The Word dwelt with God, and what God was, the Word was. The Word, then was with God at the beginning, and through him all things came to be; no single thing was created without him" (John 1:1–3). With that the council fathers could say: "we rest our case."

Unfortunately, Jesus behaved like a presidential candidate who would not mind his managers or curb his tongue. When asked about his relationship with the Father, Jesus insisted: "The Father is greater than I" (John 14:28). And that is in John's Gospel, Nicaea's best friend. From the perspective of the *homoousios* crowd, it was a major gaffe. Things went further down hill, again in John's Gospel. The people put the question of divinity to Jesus straightaway. "You, a mere man, claim to be a god." This was a silver platter opportunity to break the big news of John's Gospel and Jesus blew it away. More than that, he denied being godly in any unique way. "Is it not written in your own Law, 'I said, you are gods?' Those are called gods to whom the word of God was delivered" (John 10:34–35). Such relativizing thoughts did not play well at Nicaea and in subsequent creeds where they were studiously overlooked. Similarly unwelcome is Jesus' statement in Luke: "Why do you call me good? No one is good except God alone" (18:19). From the perspective of the councils, Jesus was not orthodox.

Nicaea and the councils that tried to mirror it lifted Jesus out of time and wafted him into eternity. The conciliar fathers took an algebraic turn. Their axiom: If Jesus was at one with the Father and the Father was eternal, *voila!* The gospels, unlike the councils, were not into algebra or Greek metaphysics. Instead they move with the freedom of poets weaving stories around this remarkable character who inspired them and inflamed their imaginations. They were not metaphysicians probing abstractions like eternity and infinity and *homoousios*. Like Jesus they had a more practical mission. Jesus' people were an occupied people wracked by poverty and beaten down by exploitation. They knew their religion, drawn from the Sinai moral-political revolution, had power that was not being marshaled to meet their current challenges, and this was at the center of their creedal gravity.

After all, disputes about the nature of Jesus' being succeeded in distracting from his moral message. Surely Constantine would prefer to talk *homoousios* than call attention to Jesus' critique of "kings [who] lord it over their subjects" (Luke 22:25). Nor would Constantine, addicted to imperial opulence, want to hear Jesus' "woe to you rich" (6:24). And he would surely not welcome Jesus' command, "Put up your sword. All who take the sword die by the sword" (Matt. 26:52), or Jesus' proclamation, "Blessed are the peacemakers" (Matt. 5:9). No, better to talk *homoousios*.

The Emperor Constantine convened the Council of Nicaea at his summer palace and invited the bishops to attend, all expenses paid. As an added lure, he even mentioned "the excellent temperature of the air." Constantine had his own agenda. He wanted to get this unsettled problem of Jesus' identity straightened out so that Christianity could better serve as cement for his sprawling empire. He had invited some fifteen hundred bishops to attend, but only three hundred accepted the invitation.[33] He got more than he bargained for when the bishops gave Jesus a divine status greater than the status of the emperor. Roman emperors also aspired to godliness, and it was bestowed on them before or after death. All of that illustrates well that god-talk is never without political implications.[34]

Imperially hosted Nicaea should have settled it. It didn't. A century and a half later at Chalcedon another council had to try to copper-fasten it. It was a loose fit and it, too, failed. By the end of the seventh century Jesus' divinity achieved a kind of shaky ascendancy. It seemed to have frozen into permanent orthodoxy but the heat of modern debates between "high Christology" and "low Christology" signals that this focal claim has never fully achieved a peaceful residence in Christianity.

CHAPTER 6

FROM JESUS TO CHRIST

There once was a man in the first century CE *who traveled from town to town, doing miracles and preaching a message of hope. It was said he cured the lame and the blind and drove out demons. He was called the "son of God" and was recognized as a prophet. He preached against greed and urged an ethic of justice and sharing. His birth was a miraculous one and his divinity was proclaimed to his mother by a heavenly messenger. There are reports that he appeared after his death.*

His name was Apollonius of Tyana.

If you expected that the name of this man would be Jesus of Nazareth you would be in the right church but the wrong pew, the right culture, but the wrong charismatic figure. This sort of thing happened in that cultural setting; neither Jesus nor Apollonius of Tyana was unique. It was all within the mythic ambience of the time.[1] You could meet gods on the street where you lived. When the Jesus people moved into the world of the Gentiles, with Paul as their main guide, they had no problem with making Jesus into a god. This bestowal of divine status was done not just for Jesus but, as A. N. Wilson says, for "Paul and the Caesars, and anyone else whom they happened to admire."[2] Claim of a virgin birth was an accepted metaphor for greatness. When the Roman philosopher Celsus wrote his critique of Christianity and its claims of a virgin birth, "he never says that such an event is incredible in itself. What is incredible is that it could happen to a member of the lower classes, a Jewish peasant nobody like Jesus."[3]

The emperor Caligula tried to have his horse declared a deity and Emperor Hadrian insisted that his dead boy-lover Antinoos be declared a god.[4] In the Acts of the Apostles we find three instances of divine "incarnation." Simon Magus was thought divine (Acts 8:14). When Paul and Barnabas were preaching in Lycaonia they so impressed the people that the crowd exclaimed: "The gods have come down to us in human form" (14:11). Barnabas, they decided, was Jupiter, and Paul was Mercury. The priests of Jupiter were so convinced of this incarnation that they brought oxen and garlands to offer sacrifice. Poor Paul and Barnabas had a devilishly hard time convincing the folks that they were "only human beings, no less mortal than you" (14:15).

What Jesus was and what was made of him are two different realities. We know this for certain, since no one person could present all the character types attributed to Jesus. No one person could be for nonviolent cheek-turning resistance one moment and then be found "drenched in blood" with a sharp sword coming out of his mouth to "smite the nations," and ruling "with an iron rod and tread the wine-press of the wrath and retribution of God" (Rev. 19:12–16). Only an unstable personality could vacillate between such polar opposites. "Jesus" was persistently refashioned to suit the literary purposes of the biblical writers.

The long effort of scholars to get past all the spin and hype to the "Jesus of history" has never been—and cannot be—a satisfying success. Anthony E. Harvey points out that we should not expect the facts of Jesus' life to have more clarity or specificity than that of "any other figure of ancient history." What we can claim to know with some certainty is that Jesus was known as a teacher in Galilee and Jerusalem, miracles were attributed to him, he was involved in controversy with fellow Jews over questions of the Law of Moses, and he was crucified under Pontius Pilate. That's it.[5] Sanders strained to find what could be called "certain or virtually certain" about Jesus, and it is a short list.[6]

Jesus Confused?

There are indications in the gospels that Jesus was confused, and in some cases plumb wrong. Confused is not a very godly thing to be. He may have shared the common conviction in his society that the world was about to come to a climactic end. Early Christians, and Jesus, too, it seems, "were expecting that the world would end soon."[7] This expectation was in the Jewish air they breathed, so it's no big surprise. There are what Hans Kung calls "several extremely inconvenient texts" asserting that Jesus expected the "kingdom of God in the imminent future." Those texts are inconvenient only if you are wed to a theory they contradict, that is, the divinity-of-Jesus theory. After talking of the grand climax of history when "the Son of Man . . . comes in the glory of his Father and of the holy angels," Jesus says, "I tell you this: there are some of those standing here who will not taste death before they have seen the kingdom of God already come in power" (Mark 8:38, 9:1). That is "extremely inconvenient" since it never happened. And it all gets worse.

Mark again records Jesus saying the big day is coming when "the sun will be darkened, the moon will not give her light; the stars will come falling from the sky, the celestial powers will be shaken. Then they will see the Son of Man coming in the clouds with great power and glory. . . . I tell you this: the present generation will live to see it all" (Mark 13:24–30). Oops. None of that happened. In Matthew's Gospel we find Jesus saying his followers will be persecuted from one town to another but "before you have gone through all the towns of Israel the son of Man will have come" (Matt. 10:23). Albert Schweitzer went so far as to say that Jesus thought the kingdom would come within a few months and saw himself as the bearer of these dramatic tidings. In these delusions, Jesus would be but a child of his times. And in his times and in his place, the mood was apocalyptic. The Aramaic-speaking, earliest Christian community in Jerusalem and possibly elsewhere in Palestine, was "expecting that the world would end soon."[8] As Leonard Shlain says: "Jesus prophesied that the end of linear time was at hand."[9] (There is so little hard data of the facts of Jesus' life, so unanimity is hard to come by. Recall that some, like Marcus J. Borg, argue that Jesus did not expect an immediate end.[10])

So there are indications that Jesus was confused and flat out wrong in his sense of history. If so, there is no indication that he saw any need to start a new religion with himself as the godly center of it. Hans Kung is in the mainstream of Christian scholarship when he says that Jesus did not want to found a church, a religion competing with his Judaism, "a special community distinct from Israel with its own creed and cult, its own constitution and ministries."[11] The community that later formed around his activities was not his doing. The eventual outreach of this religious grouping to include Gentiles was the work of Paul and others, not the work of Jesus.

Still, a community did form and whatever it was it was definitely not in the Vatican mold. Its leadership was not limited to men, and certainly not to celibate men. The apostles were married, and Jesus may have been, too. Paul regarded himself as an exception. The Jesus movement was as far as you can get from what biblical scholar Paul Hoffman calls the "dictatorial bureaucracy" that locked into place in nineteenth-century Roman Catholicism. As Elisabeth Schussler Fiorenza says of the Jesus community: "No one is exempted. Everyone is invited. Women as well as men, prostitutes as well as Pharisees."[12]

Pope Peter?

One of the most widely held views, which surfaces in the press whenever a new pope is being installed, is that Peter was the first pope and all popes are his successors—Peter being the "rock" on which the papacy stands. The idea of a juridical head of all the varied first-century movements stimulated by Jesus' life is a crude anachronism. The famous text, which has Jesus calling Peter the rock on which the church was to be built, was a later insertion into the gospel of Matthew and is found nowhere else in the New Testament. As Kung says, "it is not a saying of the earthly Jesus" but a later creation coming out of the Palestinian community.[13] Exegetically speaking, it is a loose plank for popes to stand on. There is simply no evidence that a papal monarchy can be blamed on Jesus. (If people brush off the data on the early Jesus movement and insist that Peter was appointed "pope," there would be lessons to learn. Peter was married; a married pope with a strong spouse and children—especially teenage children—would have experiences that could enrich his ministry.)

In sum, there is no evidence that Jesus founded a church as a kind of new religion separate from his Judaism. What is most likely is that he could not even imagine the possibility of such an alternative to Judaism. It is probable that he was affected by the popular expectation of the imminent consummation of human history. There would thus be no need for starting a new religion in the short time before that momentous event.

Competitive Deifications

The early Christians had a problem when they wanted to promote Jesus from merely human into the precincts of divinity. They collided with the poetic imaginings applied to other dignitaries using the metaphors and miracle claims that were common currency in those cultures. Making Jesus unique in that swelling pantheon was a hard sell. There were so many comparables and competitors. Justin Martyr, a second-century writer, noted in his *First Apology* that the Christian dogmas were not unique—and he didn't know the half of it. Perseus had also enjoyed a virgin birth. It wasn't just the Holy Spirit who could impregnate; Semele bore the offspring of Zeus. Isis, without the aid of male insemination, gave birth to her son Horus. Healing miracles were attributed to Aesculapius. The Jesus story did not monopolize resurrections. Look to the defeat of death by Ariadne, Adonis, and the Caesars. Bacchus/Dionysus suffered persecution, died, and rose from the dead. Incarnational deifications of emperors were commonplace. Some witnesses swore that they had seen Caesar ascending into heaven from the funeral pyre. With all these competing stories, it was hard to make Jesus stand out from the crowd.

Gods Dying and Eaten

Sometimes the savior god comes as a baby who is threatened by a cruel king. The myth of a dying god was found in Egypt, Mesopotamia, and Syria. Salvific sufferings of Jesus had been seen also in the stories of Gilgamesh, Heracles, and Prometheus, as well as in the "culture heroes" of Chinese mythology. Plato spoke of a "righteous man who shall be scourged, tortured, bound, his eyes burnt out, and, at last after suffering every evil, shall be impaled or crucified" (*Republic* 363 a).

The Eucharist, the central liturgy in traditional Christianity, is suspect in its origins, as something borrowed, not something new. Saint Augustine denied the real presence of Jesus in the eucharistic bread and wine. "Can the body of Christ be digested? . . . Of course not."[14] As Garry Wills writes: "Nothing is said in the first century of a 'consecration' that changed food into anything other than a sign of shared fellowship."[15] There is no indication that anyone asked at Jesus' last supper, "What just happened to the bread?"

The central rite of the Dionysiac cult was theophagy, that is, eating the god ritually. By eating the god's flesh and drinking his blood, the faithful were filled with divine power and united with the divinity. Priests of the Persian sun god Mithras prescribed ritual "washings" like baptism and also commanded "eating the flesh and drinking the blood" of their god in sacred meals.[16] The similarities got more embarrassing than Justin could have imagined when, from the fourth century on, Christians celebrated the birthday of Jesus on December 25, the birthday of the Sun god Mithra. The Mithra similarities would be unsettling for Justin and his fellow early apologists. Robin R. Meyers highlights them: "Mithra was a traveling teacher with twelve companions who was called the 'good shepherd,' 'the way, the truth, and the life,' and 'redeemer,' 'savior, and 'messiah.' He was buried in a tomb and after three days he rose again. His resurrection was celebrated every year. Mithra ascended into heaven where he offered immortality to those who had been initiated into his mysteries—by baptism . . . and the use of bread, water, and wine consecrated by priests, called 'fathers.'"[17] The similarities to Christianity so troubled Tertullian that he came up with a *devil ex machina* solution. "He tried to explain them by supposing that the devil had inspired a deliberate parody of the Christian sacraments."[18]

The myth of a dying god was found in Egypt, Mesopotamia, and Syria. The death caused negative reverberations in nature but with the god's resurrection in the spring, life was restored. Something like the salvific suffering of Jesus also appeared in the stories of Gilgamesh, Heracles, and Prometheus, as well as in the "culture heroes" of Chinese mythology.

A common Greek appearance is the young savior conceived of a god and a moral mother. The mother is persecuted and is a *mater dolorosa* (a sorrowing mother) who herself need to be saved by her son. The savior son is sometimes sacrificed like an animal to save the people and is mystically identified with some special animal such as a lamb or a bull whose sacrificed blood has special power.[19]

Sometimes the savior comes as a miraculous baby whose birth signals the dawning of a new age or kingdom. He is regularly threatened by a cruel king and usually manages to escape. The Egyptians also had the notion of a child-god and of a virgin mother who is impregnated by the spirit of a god.

The popular belief that Jesus instituted the Eucharist, making himself present in the bread and wine, at the very moment that he was present with his friends eating that same bread and drinking that same wine is, to put it mildly, counterintuitive. Add to that the theophagy precedents well known to Paul, and we see some of the borrowing that marks all geographically contiguous religions.[20]

The first three gospels might give support for Jesus as instituting the Eucharist but this raises serious problems. As A. N. Wilson says: "If we wish to believe in Jesus as the inventor of the Eucharist, or as the founder of Christianity," problems arise. We understand these three gospels to say that Jesus instituted the Eucharist at the Passover meal, but Wilson corrects: "If this is the case, then every single event which follows—the arrest of Jesus, his trial, his execution, must be a work of fiction, since it is unthinkable that the Jews would have broken their most sacred religious observances in order to put a man on trial." John's gospel puts the meal way before Passover, and, again, he has no story of Jesus instituting of the Eucharist. Wilson concludes: "The Christian Eucharist is the mystery of mysteries, feeding the hearts and imaginations of men and women for two thousand years. The great cathedrals of Europe and of the Americas were built to house it. . . . It is no small thing to recognize that it has no historical connection with Jesus of Nazareth."[21]

The ritual of sacrificing a god as is replayed in the "holy sacrifice of the Mass" was anything but unique in religious history. Indeed, as Leonard Shlain writes: "God-sacrifice with its themes of altruism, suffering, and regeneration gripped the imagination of all early peoples."[22] James Frazer in *The Golden Bough*, and Freud in *Totem and Taboo*, described sacrificial rituals used by primitives tribes to rid themselves of guilt. An animal was sacrificed, bloodily. During the feast that followed, tribe members ate the flesh and drank the blood of the sacrificed animal. This absolved all who participated from their sins. "Such rituals were common across a wide spectrum of cultures; their outlines can still be discerned in many historical belief systems. The stories of Kingu (Tiamat's son), Isiris, Dionysus, and Christ are continuations of this tradition."[23]

Early preachers of the Jesus story took two tacks to meet this onslaught of incessant look-alikes. As we saw with Tertullian, Plan A was to say they were the work of the devil who produced sham miracles to delude and distract the faithful. Plan B was to say they were *evangelica preparatio*, tone setters and stories inspired by God the Father as preparation for the true gospel, to get people ready for the real event when all of these marvels were applied to Jesus. Both Plans were a stretch too far. The evidence is straightforward: the divinity of Jesus (like Jesus himself) did not have a virgin birth. There was a lot of intercourse with ancient traditions.

Modern biblical scholarship does not turn to the devil but to history and literary criticism to distinguish fact from fiction. Catholic biblical scholar John Dominic Crossan, as an honest historian, seeks to probe beyond the "fictional overlays" that becloud the first century CE. He strives "to give an accurate but impartial account of the historical Jesus as distinct from the confessional Christ." He writes, "the Easter story at the end is, like the Nativity story at the beginning, so engraved on our imagination as factual history," when instead they are "fictional mythology." The story of Jesus' burial by his friends "was totally fictional and unhistorical. He was buried, if buried at all, by his enemies, and the necessarily shallow grave would have been easy prey for scavenging animals."[24]

But Why Did the Romans Crucify Him?

In the orthodoxy version that triumphed, Jesus was crucified as part of God's plan to have his son be a sacrificial lamb to make up for, to atone for, all the sins of all of humankind. Bloodshed is seen as salvific, as it is in all cultures relying on human and animal sacrifices to placate the gods. In this orthodoxy, the motives of the Romans were deemed irrelevant; they were but pawns in the grand and brutal atonement scheme of God the Father. Meanwhile, back in reality, the Romans crucified for a purpose. It was the Roman method of disposing of criminals, especially criminals who threatened civic order and Roman control.

The Romans did not crucify Jesus for pretensions to divinity. It was as a man, not as a god, that he bothered them. As E. P. Sanders puts it, "it is highly probable that he was executed for sedition or treason."[25] John's gospel reports: "Pilate wrote an inscription to be fastened to the cross: it read, 'Jesus of Nazareth King of the Jews.'" To stress the point, this inscription was written "in Hebrew, Latin, and Greek" (John 19:19–21). Even though he posed no military threat, kingdom talk was unsettling from the perspective of the occupiers, and it discomfited the priestly caste who benefitted from the occupation. Sanders writes: "he spoke of a kingdom and stirred the hopes of the people." His preaching "produced excitement."[26] Hope is the energy of revolution. Hope and excitement can disturb the pseudo "peace" on which tyranny depends.

The despot fears the pen of the bard more than the sword of the warrior. In times ancient and modern tyrannies seek to control the arts because the arts open minds to possibilities—and minds enlivened with possibility-consciousness are less easily controlled.

Even though Jesus associated with some violent people, it seems fairly certain that neither "he nor his disciples thought that the kingdom would be established by force of arms. They looked for an eschatological miracle."[27] There is no indication that Jesus was stupid. Taking on the power of Rome with arms would be stupid. When his companion Peter took out his sword to defend Jesus, Jesus rebuked him: "Put up your sword. All who take the sword die by the sword" (Matt. 26:52). (It is interesting that Peter was armed with a lethal weapon.) But one fact speaks loudly: the well-attested fact that the Romans executed Jesus by crucifixion indicates that he was, in a troublesome way, taking on the power of Rome. Remember, his final public act, and one that may have precipitated his death almost immediately, was his vigorous assault on the temple where he was knocking over tables and making a terrible scene (Matt. 21:12–13). This is as close to violence as we see in the Jesus story. According to John, Jesus used a weapon of sorts—he fashioned a whip of cords or rushes to use in the rout (John 2:15). Making such a ruckus in the temple did Jesus in. The temple was, in modern terms, Washington and Wall Street. An attack on such a nerve center was unforgivable.

Shortly before the attack on the temple, Jesus made a notable, indeed flamboyant, entrance into Jerusalem. It was nonviolent to be sure, though it had more in common with Michael Moore than with Gandhi. It was a subversive, challenging action; in fact, it was challenging enough to get him executed on that count alone.[28] When Caesar or his greats entered a subject city, they did so with panache, mounted on noble horses, with the people bowing before them and strewing the path with palms to demonstrate obeisance. Jesus did a sham version of this. Jesus ordered up an old donkey. His crew threw their garments on this "foal of a beast of burden," a mockery of the grand coverings of Caesar's mounts. The people put cloaks on the road and spread palms in his path shouting, "Hosanna to the Son of David," and calling him the "King of Israel."

Jesus' histrionic arrival into Jerusalem created a stir. "The whole city went wild with excitement" (Matt. 21:1–10; John 12:13). But this farcical drama was mocking Caesar's imperial grandeur. You don't mock Caesar. If you do, he crucifies you. And he did.

Saccharine Christian piety over the centuries often has portrayed Jesus as a preacher of "meek and humble" piety. Had he been that, he could have died in bed at a ripe old age. Caesar would not have needed to invoke his maximum penalty, the one reserved for rebels. As far as Caesar was concerned, Jesus could have claimed to be a god; Caesar was used to that and would have smiled, as long as he behaved and deferred to his conquerors. What Jesus did, he did as a man, not as a god. He wasn't killed for claiming divinity. As Norman Gottwald says: "The clearest single piece of historical information about Jesus is that he died as a political provocateur or disturber of that 'alliance of convenience' between the Roman occupiers and the corrupt Jewish leaders."[29]

Divinity as a Demotion

Divinizing Jesus was actually something of a put-down. From the scant information we have on his life, he seems to have been one remarkable human being. Whatever the mythology that grew up around him after his death, he was a significant figure on his own, starting in a little hamlet of some three hundred people and ending up as a major target of Caesar's wrath and a grave threat to the reigning Jewish priesthood in all their sanctimonious glory. The Roman's did not waste crucifixion on nobodies. Jesus—that probably illiterate peasant—was a somebody.[30]

Again, we cannot reach the historical person who ate and drank, lived, worked, and played in Galilee. There is evidence that he existed and his death bears witness to how disturbing he was. Beyond that, what we know is the literary and mythic construction of Jesus, "the mythopoesis of his life and death."[31] This construction may be a composite of other persons active in this community, but what we see in the person called Jesus is a shocker. Paul called him "a stumbling block to Jews and folly to Greeks," and a real "power" (1 Cor. 1:23). This yokel from poor little Nazareth shook up the learned Pharisees and the allies of Herod. He looked on them, Mark says, "with anger and sorrow at their obstinate stupidity." After encountering him, the Herodians and the Pharisees he scorned "began plotting against him . . . to see how they could make away with him" (Mark 3:5–6).

By no means does the story of Jesus depict him as the bland leading the bland. Indeed, he was courageous to the point of foolhardy. King Herod was a murderous brute. Therefore, it should have shaken Jesus' timbers when a group of distinguished Pharisees came up to him with this alarming news: "You should leave this place and go on your way; Herod is out to kill you." It was a friendly warning but Jesus blew it off with brazen gusto. He replied, "Go and tell that fox . . ." that I will keep on doing what I am doing (Luke 13:31). Here the text requires some explanation. Calling someone a fox today is only slightly demeaning. In Jesus' time it was a powerful blast. Foxes were the murderous nemesis in that pastoral society. Calling someone by that name was a capital insult. To get the flavor of the epithet translated into the parlance of our day—and I beg the reader's indulgence—Jesus was saying, "Go and tell that son of a bitch that I will keep doing what I am doing." "Fox" had all the heftiness of that modern blunt epithet. As some have said, it was not surprising that Jesus was killed. It is surprising that he was not killed sooner. His public rabbinic life lasted two, maybe three years.

The Fallacy of Misplaced Abstractness

To take this straight-talking firebrand and turn him into a "hypostatic union," as theology has done, is a sin of misplaced abstractness. To meet this iconoclastic rebel against empire and insist that his identify is explained by *circumincession*, the technical term for the interpenetration of the Three Persons in the Holy Trinity, is theology neck-high in pathetic fallacy.[32] Sartre warned against our proclivity to treat as abstract that which is concrete. The deification of Jesus is an example of such perversion—harmless abstractions replacing a concrete rebel. The flight to unrooted abstraction is an escape from the moral and political challenge of his life and death.[33] It's small wonder that the tyrannical Constantine presided over the Council at Nicaea that imposed the title *homoousios* on Jesus. That strategic spin helped neutralize the poison of rebelliousness that his short life and gory death portend to all tyrannies. All these terms were linguistic departures from the few details scholars can agree on about Jesus of Nazareth and, especially why this Jesus was executed by the Roman Empire.

From the clues that come to us about Jesus, it is no wonder that he was killed. But here is a great sadness: theology, by turning him into an abstraction, by masking his reality with "circumincession" and *homoousios*, killed him again. The real Jesus got lost. Meyers calls Jesus the Galilean Jew "the world's most famous missing person."[34] Even the famous "Lord's prayer" is central to Christian piety with little or more usually no awareness of its revolutionary bite. Crossan calls it "a prayer from the heart of Judaism on the lips of Christianity" crying out to the "conscience of the world, a radical manifesto and a hymn of hope for all humanity in language addressed to all the earth."[35] We shy from radical moral challenge just as eyes avert from the glare of the sun.

The Sequel

The revolutionary spirit of Jesus continued after his death. That is what the Easter stories are metaphorically saying. The spark he seems to have ignited stirred his followers even after his death. There was a radical core in the Jesus movement that was incompatible with the shackles of empire and this kept reasserting itself as his memory was shaped and misshaped by his successors. "Jesus is Lord" was one of the earliest proclamations of the early Jesus movement. But "Lord" was a claimed prerogative of the emperor and at the core of the cult that served as the glue for the imperium. So, too, the title "Son of God." As John Dominic Crossan and Jonathan Reed put it: "To proclaim Jesus as the Son of God was deliberately denying Caesar his highest title and to announce Jesus as Lord and Savior was calculated treason."[36] Talk of "the kingdom of God" or "of heaven" had to be very upsetting to the Romans. Even calling Jesus "Christus" was politically subversive since the term was often used to denote a ruler.[37] Claudius issued a decree banishing from Rome those Jews who were "continually raising tumults at the instigation of Chrestus" (a version of Christus).[38] Jesus made trouble for the empire before and after his death. The Ascension ascribed to Jesus was also unsettling. "If only select emperors ascended into heaven—and only those the Roman Senate considered deserving—could the proclamation of the ascension of Jesus have been harmless?"[39] (But note again, ascensions were run-of-the-mill for prestigious persons.)

The Art of Subversion

It is doubtful that Jesus and Paul could have a comfortable conversation together. Jesus and Gandhi, however, could have a meeting of minds. It is arguable that Jesus, like Gandhi, was a nonviolent subversive, working to undermine imperial occupation by nonviolent resistance. Both were enemies of the TINA (There Is No Alternative) mind-set. One text, perhaps the most misunderstood text in the Christian scriptures, shows a master subversive at work. It shows Jesus as an early pioneer in the art of nonviolent but active resistance.

About Turning That Other Cheek

The gospel text that is so well known and so rarely understood is this:

> If someone slaps you on the right cheek, turn and offer him your left. If a man wants to sue you for your shirt, let him

> have your coat as well. If a man in authority makes you go one mile, go with him two. (Matt. 5:38–41)

As it is all too commonly understood, this text is, as Walter Wink says, often became "the basis for systematic training in cowardice, as Christians are taught to acquiesce to evil."[40] Cowardice is not a virtue. Even Gandhi said that if there were only two choices, cowardice or violence, he would choose violence. This text has been used to say that the Christian response to oppression is submission. Wives should "turn the other cheek" and defer to an abusive spouse. Citizens should submit to despots and walk the extra mile beyond what they are unreasonably asked to do so. When you are robbed, give even more to the robber who just stole your shirt.

As Wink says, "human evolution has provided the species with two deeply instinctual responses to violence: flight or fight. Jesus offers a third way: nonviolent direct action."[41]

Text without context is a crapshoot; you might get what it means but you probably won't. With biblical expert Wink as our guide, here is why this text had the political dynamite that could get you crucified.

Turning the other Cheek

In that culture, as Wink explains, the only way you could slap someone on the right cheek would be with the back of the hand. This had a meaning in that culture. It did not signal a fistfight between equals; its purpose was not to injure but to humiliate. Slapping a peer in this manner brought on serious penalties, but doing it to a slave was not penalized. It was meant to humiliate and discipline slaves and those of inferior rank. The people to whom Jesus spoke experienced these insults. They were an occupied people and they were regularly slapped, stripped of their goods, and forced to perform services against their will.

So why then would Jesus counsel an already downtrodden and abused people to turn the other cheek? The struck person was announcing to the striker that the slap has failed in its purpose. It did not humiliate or bring shame. The victim, his dignity intact, turns the cheek and calmly invites more, and by so doing he renders the slapper impotent, frustrated in his desire to make the victim crawl. As Gandhi said: "The first principle of nonviolent action is that of non-cooperation with everything humiliating."[42] Turning the other cheek in this context is not passive; it is "non-cooperation," an act of disarming, nonviolent resistance.

Getting Sued for Your Clothing

Only the very poor could get sued for their clothing, implying that they had nothing else to offer as collateral. The two garments in the text are the outer garment or cloak and the inner garment. In this brutal system of debt-recovery, the creditor could leave the debtor with only his undergarment. When reduced to this, Jesus says, strip off your inner garment, too, and give that also to the creditor. In that culture nakedness was taboo. Anyone seeing someone naked was more shamed than the naked person (Gen. 9:20–27). Jesus' advice was to say in effect, "Since your greed would take the coat I need for warmth, then here, take my underwear and finish the job and let all see what you are doing to the poor of this land." Once again it is active nonviolent resistance, not acquiescence to evil. And you would probably get your clothes back.

Walk the Extra Mile

The occupiers assumed the right to requisition people to do chores for them. In this case a Roman soldier was permitted by law to force you to carry his pack—which might weigh up to 80 pounds—but by law he was only allowed to force you for one mile. This limit was put in place to minimize resentment and soldiers could be punished for demanding more. If he makes a citizen carry his pack, then the soldier must take his pack back at the mile marker under fear of penalty. So Jesus recommends saying to the soldier, "No, I will carry it further." As Wink puts it: "Imagine the situation of a Roman infantryman pleading with a Jew to give back his pack. The humor of this scene may have escaped us, but it could scarcely have been lost on

Jesus' hearers, who must have been regaled at the prospect of thus discomfiting their oppressors."[43] Again, there is no violence here but there is resistance, and there is empowerment.

We see this same tactic in modern times in the Danes who did not resist the Nazi invasion but who would regularly march in quiet peaceful dignity following their king. Sometimes they would sing Danish anthems and, with some exception, their response to the invasion was nonviolent. They were saying to their occupiers: you have occupied our nation but you have not occupied or conquered our spirits.

When Jesus advocated nonviolent active resistance, he emboldened his hearers. He was antidotal to the numbed immobility of the cowed. He was dangerous, not as a god, but as a person with a passionate sense of justice. And as a person, not as a god, he had to be killed. It was not an angry Father God who demanded his death as propitiation for the sins of humankind. It was Rome that did the killing and Rome did not visit crucifixion on deluded religious preachers. It was reserved for first-class troublemakers and Jesus seems to have qualified.

CHAPTER 7

FROM CHRISTIANITY TO CROSS-TIANITY

A cynical advertiser once said, "Show me your zip code and I'll tell you what you eat, drink, wear, watch, and drive." Better yet, show me your god and I will have a window into your society and its culture. God-talk and culture are interlocutors with constant interface; change in one is reflected in the other. What does this mean for Jesus? As soon as he was divinized, he was subject to identity theft. There is no point in complaining; it happens to all the gods. Gods function mainly as mirrors, reflecting what that society has become—and, at times, reflecting a society's moral hungers and ideals. Faux secular sophisticates take heed! Gods are creatures and they reflect their creators' virtues and vices. They should never be bypassed in sociological analysis.

Theists like to ascribe immutability to their gods. There is no encomium the gods deserve less; they are mutants one and all. As history swirls and changes, so, too, do its gods. But whatever of their identity shifts, the gods are powerful motivating forces. Once the society forms them, the gods get drafted into service. Practical people with a mission know this and always harness the gods to their purposes. The Crusaders did this. They turned their god into what they themselves were, a bloodthirsty demon. Then they could shout *Deus vult* to propel their forces to slaughter. Hitler could emblazon *Gott mi uns* on the buckles of his troops and the Conquistadores tore into the "open veins" of "Latin" America with the cross on their flags and armor.[1] As Alfred North Whitehead said: "The church gave unto God the attributes which belonged exclusively to Caesar."[2] And so it goes.

The Pains and Gains of God-Making

Should Jesus have claimed to be god—and there is no evidence that he ever did—he would have found ample evidence of what fate awaited him in his Bible, the Hebrew scriptures. Those writings are a textbook on the symbiosis of gods and social movements. In the mono-Yahwism of ancient Israel, there was, as Norman K. Gottwald puts it, "a rich field of correlations with numerous functional interlocks between the religion and the society. . . . All of the symbols of Yahweh in his various guises refer with positive reinforcements to socioeconomic desiderata in the community and to the assurance that power will be used in ways that preserve the system externally and internally."[3]

The quote from Norman Gottwald is a mouthful; note carefully what it says. Yahweh has "various guises" confected by that society for very practical purposes. Yahweh is assigned the role of reinforcing "the socioeconomic desiderata" of that community. His job is to preserve the system and ensure order. Bringing Yahweh in on this was smart because clout was added as the community's needs then become "divine law." When the law is not just law, but God's law, you pick up not just prestige but also persuasive power. If the thundering and flashing god of the mountain wants it, the people had best take heed.

Unlike neighboring gods, Yahweh was not interested in life after death or ancestor worship. He was mainly a community organizer. He was a multitasker. For example, he was also a "man of war," a commander in chief rousing folks to battle when war was the perceived need. At his best in early Israel, Yahweh was protector of a noble, prescient socioeconomic experiment; his job was to secure "the integrity of the egalitarian community" that ancient Israel was innovating.[4]

What we see here is not God creating humans "in his image and likeness," but a precocious community creating God in its image and likeness, and commanding him to keep it going. Israel was struggling to become "a self-governing association of economically self-sufficient free farmers and herdsmen constituting a single class of peoples with common ownership of the means of production vested in large families."[5] It took a "God"—and an active one—to keep that show on the road. (The etymological root of "Yahweh" implies "one who makes things happen," and this experiment was one large happening. Nothing less than godly energies would do.) This sociopolitical egalitarianism in Israel put it at odds with the hierarchic centralized rules of neighboring city-states in that general area, and this often led to war. So protecting this egalitarian society was "job one" for Yahweh and puts him in a better light than some of the other "guises" invented and choreographed for him at other times.

Seeds of Democratic Theory

This system Yahweh was to protect was a first glimmering of democratic rule. It "depended greatly on consensual understanding of and commitment to common interests, requiring, as it were, the ancient tribal equivalent of 'an enlightened and publicly active citizenry.'"[6] The feisty tribes of Yahweh were enlightened enough to know that unlimited wealth wreaks "violence" (Micah 6:12) and is always shielded by lies and deceit, an insight that stands out in its enduring contemporaneity.

Yahweh and the people who crafted him were stubborn pioneers in early democracy. As Gottwald asks: "What other instances do we possess from the ancient Near East of the underclasses from a feudal society overthrowing their lords and living in an egalitarian social system over a wide area of formerly feudalized land for two centuries" before succumbing to monarchy?[7] He knows of none, and his reach is far and wide.

This was one of the high points of Yahweh's career. He was not, subsequently, always so nice or so high-minded. When you are made in the image and likeness of a people you are going to have ups and downs. In a fearsome chapter of Torah, Deuteronomy 13, Yahweh takes a sociopathic turn. One minute he is into love-talk, though in a self-centered sort of way, demanding that the people love "the Lord your God with all your heart and soul." He then descends into sick fury, jealousy, and violence. If any member of your family dares to get a little ecumenical and flirts with other gods, you must stone to death that son or daughter or relative of yours. And if you conquer a city that is aligned with other gods, you must kill all its inhabitants, gather all its goods into the square, and burn both the city and everything in it "as a complete offering to the Lord your God." (This is an interesting admission that the people make the gods; eliminate the people and the gods are toast.) If you do all that holy mayhem, God will increase your numbers and lead you on to happy times. Not nice.

So, is God brutal? Or is God egalitarian and progressive? It all depends on the society's shifting needs. For Tacitus, the gods were with the mighty. That made good imperial sense to the Romans. When the early tribes of Yahweh pioneered an egalitarian society that favored the poor over the rich (more on that in Part IV), their god became a "God of justice" (Isa. 30:18), described by Judith as a "God of the humble . . . the poor . . . the weak . . . the desperate . . . and the helpless" (Jud. 9:11). Strange credentials indeed for a god, but perfectly reflective of the revolutionary mood of early Israel.

All this means that Jesus, in the godly guises to be imposed on him, can expect more of the personality transplants that all the gods endured.

In sum, the Hebrew gods show two things: (1) the people make the gods, not the other way around; and, (2) those gods have social functions. They can have a long shelf life and can be invoked centuries after their creation to prod folks to evil as with the Crusaders or Christian anti-Semites. Or they can be summoned to call people back to their better moments as the prophets of Israel did. These prophetic movers and shakers put words like these into the mouth of God: "I remember the unfailing devotion of your youth, the love of your bridal days, when you followed me in the wilderness, through a land unsown," when we pioneered together an egalitarian just society and dreamt dreams of peace unparalleled in history (Jer. 2:2).

Jesus' Trek through History

When it came to writing about Jesus and shaping his literary image, Paul was the first one out of the gate, and it was a powerful pen he brought to the mission. It is a mistake to say Paul founded Christianity. No single individual ever founds a religion. But no other individual was so influential as Paul in shaping the Jesus story that morphed into church. He wrote his letters before the gospels were written, influencing the synoptic gospel writers. With eloquent strokes of his mighty pen, he sketched the lineaments of the Jesus we all came to know, a Jesus, by the way, that Jesus himself would not have recognized. Western Christianity is, to a significant degree, Pauline. Paul's epistle to the Romans has been called "one of the most influential books ever written." It had life-changing effects on influential people like Augustine, Luther, and Calvin, "and could therefore be said to be one of the key books to understanding the intellectual and social development of the Western world."[8]

There is more than a bit of irony in Paul's ascendant position in Christian history. He was not orthodox—meaning he was a heretic by the doctrinal standards that later came to prevail. He did not believe Jesus preexisted from all eternity as one of the persons of the Triune God.[9] This does get complicated. If Paul was a heretic, then is the Christianity he was influential in shaping also heretical? The fact is that this prime architect of Christian doctrine was in many ways more Jewish than Christian—especially regarding Jesus' status—since Paul always saw Jesus as subordinate to God and therefore not *homoousios*.[10] Paul also was confused about the imminent return of Jesus. He expected it. To read Paul is to enter the land of "oops."

Bloodshed as Salvific

What Paul did lock in—very successfully and very sadly—was the idea of atonement, the idea that Jesus' main mission was to atone through his death for the sinfulness of all humankind. Paul wrote to the Corinthians that his faith rested entirely on "Christ, and him crucified," on Christ nailed to the cross (1 Cor. 2:2). Paul gave a supremely positive meaning to the disgrace of the cross. We are a sinful people. Debts are to be paid to God for our sins. The heavy debt we owed was transferred to the account of Jesus and his death paid all our bills. "Christ died for us while we were yet sinners, and that is God's own proof of his love towards us" (Rom. 5:8). So the day Jesus got crucified was, to be sure, one really terrible day for Jesus, but for us it was an epic of God's love. "We have now been justified by Christ's sacrificial death" and, what's more, we shall all the more certainly be saved through him from final retribution. We have been "reconciled" to God "through the death of his Son" (5:9–11). For us it's a deal and a half. For Jesus, not so much. It was a God-awful day for him.

But it was a good day for Paul—he would approve of calling it Good Friday—because this scheme he concocted eased his neurotic sense of guilt. Paul would have agreed with Freud on how crippling feelings of guilt can be. Jesus' crucifixion was Paul's therapy and Christianity's unhappy legacy.

The early Christians did have a problem. The central figure of their faith was executed by the Romans in the most savage way the Romans could devise. The body of the crucified was left hanging on the cross as a poster boy to other potential rebels, to be eaten by the wild birds and animals. (The gospel story of the gentle care given to Jesus' quickly removed crucified body is dubious.) The early followers of Jesus did not go about making crucifixes. Indeed the first carved cross appeared in the seventh century and it showed a triumphant resurrected Jesus. It was not until the tenth century that we find a realistic carving of Jesus on the cross, the Gero Cross now in the Cologne Cathedral.

The cross, for early Christians, was no more central to their art than would be an electric chair if a modern religious reformer died that way. We could not imagine the high altar of such a religion with a replica of an electric chair atop the altar or little electric chair images to be worn on a necklace. No, the faithful would shrink in horror from the fate of their revered leader. And that is what

Christian art did. But not Paul. Paul grabbed the cross and mysticalized it, reaching into the history of blood sacrifice as atonement for sin. The Jewish sacrifice of the lamb became the model for the Roman execution of Jesus who became the "lamb of God," who died to take the rap for all of us.

The atonement narrative turns God the Father into a sadist who needed the gory death of his innocent son to make him feel better about the sins of everybody else. There were other strained efforts in the Christian Bible to deal with the embarrassment of Jesus' dreadful death. Mark tried out the idea of having Jesus "give his life as a ransom for many" (Mark 10:45). This weird idea is echoed in Timothy 2:4 and Revelation 5:9, and it appealed to a number of later luminaries including Origen, Athanasius, and Augustine.

As Bible scholar Robert Bruce McLaren says, look at this alibi for a moment and it implodes into absurdity.[11] To whom is the ransom paid? If it is to be paid to Satan, don't we then have "God the Father" put in a position of bargaining with this demigod? If we follow this story line, "God the Father" looks a bit shady. After giving Jesus as ransom, God tricks this Satan fellow by raising Jesus from the dead in three days. A classical "bait and switch" deception. Neither Luke nor John got on board this ransom theory, but the theory kept popping up for centuries until the eleventh and twelfth centuries when it faded. Anselm's *Cur Deus Homo?* put it away and atonement seemed triumphant. For a time it was, and it still lives, in explanations of the Eucharist as "the holy sacrifice of the Mass" in the Catholic and high church traditions. However, the idea of transferring the guilt of one person to another has been well thrashed, even by philosophers such as Immanuel Kant, and more benign theories have been fancied.[12]

The Fish That Got Away

The fish was a favored symbol of the faith in early Christianity. Partly this was due to how the Greek letters for the word *fish* provided a convenient pneumonic for faith claims about Jesus, but also because it lent an air of conviviality. Jesus asked to be remembered at a festive meal and a fish could be at the center of such a repast. But the fish lost out to the cross. There are no steeples with a fish image on top and fish are not featured on the altar or on the vestments of the clergy. The cross instead became the master symbol of Christianity and it has a sorry history. It is ensconced atop tombstones, steeples, and worship sites, and people "cross themselves" with a hand gesture to begin their rituals and prayers.

That's a shame because the elevation of the cross insinuated the persistent myth that violence is salvific. The fish was gentle; the cross is not. In very short order the cross became a symbol of war. Constantine was told, "*In hoc signo vinces*"—in this sign, this cross, will you conquer. As the story is told, he ordered his soldiers to paint a cross on their shields. And, unfortunately, he won. The military and imperial career of the cross was launched and war was sacralized. And Jesus himself received a big personality transplant. Christian nations would go on to sport the cross in their war medals—the Iron Cross in Germany, the Victoria Cross in Britain, the St. George Cross in Russia, and the Cross of the League of Honor in France.

As Jurgen Moltmann said, "the enemies of the Christian empire became the enemies of God. Wars became 'holy wars,' military campaigns became 'crusades,' and whoever gave his life in the battles became a martyr and his death a sacrifice."[13] Christians were "born again," but this time as killers. The Christian martyrs so revered early on were supplanted by the soldiers. St. George, an actual Christian martyr killed by the Roman empire around 304 CE, was transfigured in mythology into a military hero of the new Christian empire of Constantine. Again Moltmann: "the death of the soldier received a religious halo, and it was sanctified and glorified by the understanding that they died that we may live. They died for us."[14] They were the new Christs and the cross of Jesus will adorn their graves. There were no more victims among the soldiers who died in the charges of light and heavy brigades. They were now holy heroes of this new religious militarism, part of the holy sacrifice of war. Soldiers now marched in lockstep with God. "God is marching on" sang the Battle Hymn of the Republic (sung most recently in the National Cathedral after 9/11). And that marching God, like early Yahweh, "loosed the fateful lightning of his terrible swift sword." No patsy he. No wimpy god for Constantinian Christianity!

How Easily Things Are Broken

Early Christians thought themselves the vanguard of the age of peace predicted by the Hebrew prophets. For nearly three hundred years the chorus of their writers was almost unanimously antiwar. Origen said Christians should beware lest "for war, or for the vindication of our rights or for any occasion, we should take out the sword, for no such occasion is allowed by this evangelical teaching."[15] Tertullian was equally unambiguous: "Christ in disarming Peter disarmed every soldier."[16] Lactantius, the eloquent Christian Cicero, said as late as 304 CE that "participation in warfare therefore will not be legitimate for a just man."[17] Granted that the *Pax Romana* made it easier for this kind of idealism to flourish, it was a sincerely held conviction. Roland Bainton says that "the outstanding writers of the East and the West repudiated participation in warfare for Christians."[18]

But then a big/funny thing happened on the way to the promised land of peace. In 312 came the Constantinian turn, Constantine suddenly finding Christianity to be useful for his purposes. Christians leaped from persecution to preferment, and a heady wine it was. It sent these former peace people reeling. Constantine sent his armies out to discipline religious dissidents. Eusebius the historian was beside himself with glee at the idea of a "Christian" emperor: "The God of all, the supreme governor of the whole universe by his own will appointed Constantine."[19]

Eusebius took it in stride that Constantine was now chastening the "adversaries of the truth with the usages of war." Lactantius who spoke so grandly about nonviolent Christianity was positively giddy as he rejoiced that divine providence could have appointed so superior a person "as its agent and minister."[20] Music to Constantine's ears! Nobody was rushing to beat this friendly sword into a plowshare. The Christian peace movement took an ignoble detour.

And the divine Jesus? Was he, like other gods, a rapid change artist? Yes. He was given a military makeover. Very quickly he became active in his new role as warlord. One of his battle feats shows that he was not just tough, he was versatile. He came up with a kind of fourth-century weapon of mass destruction using biological weaponry. He also brought a touch of buffoonery to the grimness of war.

A fourth-century bishop on Nisibis reported that in a battle with the Persians, Jesus routed the enemy by sending a dense cloud of mosquitoes and gnats to tickle the trunks of the enemy's elephants and the nostrils of his horses. Hard to run an army when your elephants and horses are running around sneezing and scratching and trying to shake off clouds of hungry mosquitoes.

And so it came to pass that the noble effort to put Isaiah's dream of peace into action folded. The Christian abhorrence and avoidance of military service faded so fast that by 416 you had to be a Christian to serve in the Roman army according to the Theodosian Code. One of the pastoral problems of the day came from men saying they were Christians just to get in the army. The Canons of St. Hippolytus stipulated that a catechumen (someone preparing for baptism) who showed military ambitions was to be rejected because this "is far from the Lord."[21] That was that Lord and that was then—not the Jesus being born again as a warrior in the fourth century.

Since war was now respectable, writers such as Augustine and Ambrose baptized the just-war concepts rooted in Greco-Roman thinkers such as Plato and Cicero. Christians could go to war, said Augustine, but only in a mournful mood. His position was more redolent of the library than the battlefield when he wrote: "Love does not exclude wars of mercy waged by the good."[22] Thus does theory again display itself as a faithful acolyte to the regnant powers.

The "just war theory" with its efforts to put some brakes on war was quickly drowned in the wave of violence that swept over the declining Roman empire. The *Pax Romana* buckled and the so-called barbarians arrived. Many of them were impressed by Roman achievements and also by Christianity. They converted in droves but the waters of baptism did not wash away the violence that suffused their existence. Arriving into Christianity, they joined in the rewriting of both Jesus and the religion that had formed around his memory. St. Michael with his sword replaced Wotan, their god of war. They loved the story of Peter in the garden pulling out the sword and slashing off the ear of the High Priest's servant. They ignored Jesus' rebuke.

In subsequent centuries, "just war" strictures quickly became an irrelevant abstraction and Christendom sank into a cauldron of violence. In a well-meaning but hopeless effort to stem the tide of violence, the church leaders in the tenth century instituted the Truce of God. The terms of the Truce are pathetically revealing. The Truce banned all killing for several months around the feast of Easter, for four weeks before Christmas, and on all Fridays, Sundays, and holy days, of which there were many. Church properties and the clergy were always to be exempt from violence. The clergy were making the rules! Also immunity was extended to peasants, pilgrims, agricultural animals, and olive trees.

If the laws of the Truce were to be honored, it would have been difficult to know without a calendar and good interviewing skills who you could kill and when. How would one prove that he was a bona fide peasant or pilgrim and how did pigs and olive trees get involved in all this?

In the ultimate and most revealing irony, everyone from the age of twelve upward was bound to take an oath to obey the Truce and those who would refuse to do so were to be killed.[23] (We see shadows of this oxymoronic perversion in our day as "pro-life" terrorists murder physicians.)

The futility of the Truce shines forth in the form of the oath taken by Robert the Pious. The sobriquet "Pious" would seem to suggest he was a cut above his peers in virtue. But what a cagey fellow his oath shows him to have been. He is a master of excusing provisos: "I will not burn houses or destroy them, unless there is a knight inside" (arson was apparently one of pious Robert's weapons of choice); "I will not root up vines" (he doesn't qualify this; Robert was not a vine-rooter-upper sort of person); "I will not attach noble ladies nor their maids nor widows or nuns, unless it is their fault" (there are escape clauses galore in that promise; who determines which ladies are "noble" and what due process is used in assigning "fault?" At any rate, attacking ladies does not *per se* offend Robert's piety); "From the beginning of Lent to the end of Easter I will not attack an unarmed Knight."[24] (Enough said.)

As Windass said: "The disease was too radical to respond to such first aid."[25] And all of this in a culture and political economy called "Christendom," named in cruel irony for none other than Jesus. When this band-aid failed to cure the malignancy Christendom had become, church leaders decided to divert the "bellicosity to a foreign adventure." With that the Crusades were born. Pope Urban II at the Council of Clermont in 1095 sounded the call. Employing racism as a stimulant, His Holiness told the faithful, "You are obligated to succor your brethren in the East, menaced by an accursed race, utterly alienated from God. The Holy Sepulcher of our Lord is polluted by the filthiness of an unclean nation. . . . Start upon the road to the Holy Sepulcher to wrest that land from the wicked race and subject it to yourselves."[26]

The faithful responded with gusto. The debacle lends more support for the poet Alexander Pope's observation: "the worst of madmen is a saint gone mad." A text from Jeremiah became a favorite: "Cursed be he that keepeth back his hand from blood." Bohemond of Antioch sent to the Greek Emperor a whole cargo of noses and thumbs sliced from the Saracens. The "just war theory" and the Truce of God" were nowhere in sight. Raymond of Agile gave the following account of what happened in the capture of Jerusalem:

> Some of our men (and this was more merciful) cut off the heads of their enemies; others shot them with arrows, so that they fell from the towers; others tortured them longer by casting them into the flames. Piles of head, hands, and feet are to be seen in the streets of the city. It was necessary to pick one's way over the bodies of men and horses. But these were small matters compared to what happened at the temple of Solomon, a place where religious services are ordinarily chanted. What happened there? If I tell the truth, it will exceed your powers of belief. So let it suffice to say this much at least, that in the temple and portico of Solomon men rode in blood up to their knees and the bridle reins. Indeed, it was a just and splendid judgment of God that this place should be filled with the blood of unbelievers, when it had suffered to long from their blasphemies.
>
> This day, I say marks the justification of all Christianity and the humiliation of paganism; our faith was renewed. The Lord made this day and we rejoiced and exulted in it for on this day the Lord revealed Himself to His people and blessed them.[27]

Violence, earlier deemed incompatible with Christianity had become a sacrament. And this religiously grounded bellicosity is not just of historical interest. As anthropologist Alice Beck Kehoe says, it created "an ethos that continues to activate millions of our fellow citizens. . . . To understand today's militant Christian Right requires history, sociological analysis, semantics, and basic anthropological concepts to develop an understanding of this powerful American subculture."[28]

Safety in Atheism?

Though a saint gone mad may be the worst of madmen, there are other madmen and other addicts of kill-power. The roots of war are deeper than the theism-atheism philosophies. Karen Armstrong reminds us, "Nietzsche's theories were used by a later generation of Germans to justify the policies of National Socialism, a reminder that an atheistic ideology can lead to just as cruel a crusading ethic as the idea of 'God.'"[29] War has deeper roots than do the gods. Only in 8 percent of history do we find that humans have not been killing one another.[30] Erich Fromm notes that the human being "is the only mammal who is a large-scale killer and sadist."[31] We, the creators of gods, cannot blame our divine children for the festering flaws in our own nature—mirrored in them, our artifacts.

PART III

THE LIVING DEAD

CHAPTER 8

FROM HELL TO JIGGLEDEEGREEN

Afterlife is more popular than "God."

As John Dewey observed: "Many persons and movements allied with historic religion have made immortality more important than the existence of God, and indeed have conceived God's existence to be important chiefly as a warrant for personal continuance."[1] Even many Buddhists, who are, in the main, nontheistic, do not see death as the end of life: it is transitional from one state to another, not unlike the Catholic funeral liturgy, *vita mutatur, non tollitur*, life is changed, not taken away.

Afterlife belief is *otherworldly* in the strict sense. It postulates another parallel but invisible world to which the dead go leaving their dead bodies here. In Buddhism, for example, William R. LaFleur, writing on Japanese Buddhism, says that when a child is born there is a belief that it "has not appeared entirely *de novo*. . . . Although many Japanese, especially in modern times, prefer to be somewhat imprecise about the 'preexistence' of the fetus or newborn, there is, in keeping with Buddhism, a vague sense that a life that appears in our world or in a woman's uterus is the re-formation of a being that was before either in *this* world in other incarnations or in the world of the *kami*, or gods."[2]

This otherworldly mythology has practical import for some Buddhists in dealing with abortion. It allows them to imagine that the fetus is not being killed. The *mizuko*, the being that was about to be born had abortion not intervened, is not eliminated, just put on hold. "For the parent who wants to imagine its deceased or aborted *mizuko* as potentially coming back to be reborn into the same family at a time more convenient for all concerned, referring to its 'return' can imply that although it is being sent back to another world for a period of waiting, it is fully expected to be reincarnated into this world—and perhaps even this family!—at some later date. In that sense the aborted fetus is not so much being 'terminated' as it is being put on 'hold,' asked to bide its time in some other world."[3]

Since Buddhism grew out of Indian culture where belief in reincarnation was broadly held, Buddhism could hardly escape it. Many modern Buddhists, however, can and do escape it. As David Loy points out, in the India where the Buddha first taught, belief in karma and rebirth were pervasive and the Buddha was not immune to this culturally ensconced belief. The Buddha even spoke of remembering his past lifetimes. This belief is not taken as essential to Buddhism. As to the Buddha's past-life recollections, Buddhist scholar Loy says: "Perhaps a contemporary equivalent is the adult recovery of childhood memories—some of which are later discovered to be false."[4]

This inability of even the most creative thinker to escape the gripping myths of the culture applies to all religions, including Christianity. Erich Fromm's comments on the revolutionary thinking of Sigmund Freud have application to the history of religions:

> The attempt to understand Freud's theoretical system, or that of any creative systematic thinker, cannot be successful unless we recognize that, and why, every system as it is developed and presented by its author is necessarily erroneous . . . the creative thinker must think in the terms of the logic, the thought patterns, the expressible concepts of his culture. That means he has not yet the proper words to express the creative, the new, the liberating idea. He is forced to solve an insoluble problem to express the new thought in concepts and words that do not yet exist in his language. . . . The

> consequence is that the new thought as he formulated it is a blend of what is truly new and the conventional thought which it transcends. The thinker, however, is not conscious of this contradiction.[5]

Afterlife-thinking emerged out of a culture packed tight with afterlife convictions. For Christianity, as for Buddhism, we have to seek out what new thought might be there wrapped in old fabrics.

Imagination Unbound

Afterlife imaginings need not file a flight plan. Since no human being ever had experience of an afterlife in some other "world," imagination is free to construct fictive afterlife scenarios *ad libitum*. Such fantasies can be benign or malignant. The Japanese Buddhists who relegate the "being about to be born" to a pleasant waiting area consoles the bereaved parent and is benign. The medieval Christians' use of imagining hell and purgatory as postmortem torture that cast you into the volcano of Mt. Etna was a malignant and sociopathic way of urging people to live a good life or else. In either case we are dealing with imagination and myth, with no limit placed on inventiveness. It is characteristic of religious people to see immediately that the afterlife images of other peoples are mythic and made up, whereas their own are well-grounded and numinously endorsed.

The variety of afterlife fantasies, however, illumines the psychological genealogy of afterlife hypotheses. Belief in survival after death is persistent and varied and seems as old as the species. As Robert Wright says, there was "always an afterlife in hunter-gatherer religion."[6] However, it often had little or nothing to do with morality. It was not in the genre of "the good go to a nice place, the bad go straight to hell." Indeed, how you died did more to determine your afterlife fate than how you had lived. Many Andaman Islanders believed that if you drowned you would become a sea spirit, maybe even a killer whale. The jungle would be your residence if you died on land. Whether you were a good boy or a bad boy mattered not.

The Bible on Afterlife

The Hebrew Bible, Jesus' Bible, is not helpful to Christian afterlife hypotheses. Alan Richardson notes: "Early Hebrew thought had no adequate conception of a spiritual survival after death."[7] That did change but only at the very end of the biblical period would there be any idea of life with a deity after death.[8] The dead went to *Sheol*, which was pretty much the grave writ large, and there was nothing heavenly about it. *Sheol* is sometimes translated as "the grave" or "the Pit." The Hebrews did not think of death as a total extinction but as an underworld of shadows and misery. At times, as in Psalm 39, death teeters on the edge of nothingness, as when the psalmist begs for a blessing "before I go away and cease to be" (v. 13). Dennis Nineham puts it this way: "Broadly speaking, the Jews of the Old Testament period did not believe in life after death at all."[9]

In Hebraic thinking, as Jon Davies puts it, "The strength of the dread of idolatry and the necessity of maintaining the inscrutability of God remains as the major reason for restraining a too explicit view of life after death, and in particular the expectation of individual resurrection."[10] There was a fear of lapsing into the Canaanite veneration of spirits and ghosts.

Under varying influences, including the need for postmortem vindication of virtue and punishment for persecutors, afterlife hopes began to appear. Isaiah seems to endorse life after death: "But thy dead live, their bodies will rise again. They that sleep in the earth will awake and shout for joy, and the earth will bring those long dead to birth again" (26:19). Some experts think the text is figurative of a crushed people rising again and not a statement on life prospects after death. The book of Daniel gives the clearest statement of resurrection and life after death: "Many of those who sleep in the dust of the earth will wake; some to everlasting life and some to the reproach of eternal abhorrence" (12:1–2). And yet the venerable and long-suffering Job was a skeptic. The gifted author of the Book of Job, who was both a poet and a philosopher, offers sophisticated mockery of afterlife belief. "If a man dies," he asks, "can he live again?" That puts the question squarely, and he replies: "He shall never be roused from this sleep." He will disappear "as a river shrinks and runs dry." After death he will have no knowledge of what is going on in life. "His sons rise to honor, and he sees nothing of it" (Job: 14:21).

Clearly there was more Jewish interest in an afterlife from the second century BCE. Davies says it has assumed "a central position from the second century BCE although there was powerful resistance to such an idea in both Jerusalem and Samaria. . . . The general expectation of an afterlife is most clearly stated in Sanhedrin in both the Mishnah and in the Babylonian Talmud." However, there is a proviso. Evil nonrighteous people "are to be excluded from the general resurrection."[11] So resurrection involves a meritocracy. Immortality is not natural. Only the righteous get it; others, as Job would put it, are like a river that "shrinks and runs dry." Disbelief in an afterlife is thus, one biblical point of view, coexisting with belief in some sort of after-death living.

Something Borrowed, Something New

Once again, beliefs and myths do not arise from a contextual void. Nothing is intelligible outside its history said the Jesuit paleontologist Teilhard de Chardin, and that includes religious dogmas like afterlife. When Herod Antipas heard of Jesus condemning adultery, he thought that John the Baptist has returned from the grave to torment him. Resurrection was a plausible happening in that culture.

Luke has the story of a nasty rich man named Dives, a biblical Ebenezer Scrooge. He lived in wealth and showed no compassion for the poor. He was cast like old Marley into Hades and there became aware of how the poor he scorned were basking in the embrace of Abraham in heaven. He wanted to warn his relatives so they would not share his fate.

Luke was not being original when he penned this parable. He was borrowing from a tale in the "Egyptian Book of the Dead," from the second millennium BCE about a rich man repenting his sins in the court of Osiris. Again it shows the emergence of what Robert Wright calls "morally contingent afterlife," afterlife prospects used as discipline in this life. This came to be the standard perception in the Christian story.

Problems with Resurrected Bodies

With Jews, afterlife stories necessarily involved bodily resurrection since they understood a person as a living body. A drastic manifestation of this belief is in the story of Razis in 2 Maccabees. Mortally wounded Razis "took his entrails in both hands and flung them at the crowd. And thus, invoking the Lord of life and breath to give those entrails back to him again, he died" (14:45–46). So Razis fully expected a resurrection of his body with all of its parts restored.

In any age, bodily resurrection raises many conundrums and concerns. If someone had a cosmetic nose adjustment, would they arise with their original nose or the more aesthetic one wrought by the cosmetic surgery? The question of teeth also arises. Would all the resurrected saints have a full mouthful of healthy teeth? What age would we be when resurrected? One would hope we would not rise old and wracked by cancer and stroke, the terrible diseases that brought about our death. However, it would certainly be best if all do not arise as teenagers. A heaven full of only teenagers could be seriously lacking in serenity.

In the middle ages, some held that the resurrected dead would all return at age thirty, Jesus' age at the resurrection.[12] Effigies on tombs often portrayed the resurrected person at this age. None were pictured as teenagers. And what of those who died as infants? Would they stay that way in the afterlife? If they were upgraded to age thirty, would they be truly human, lacking as they would, a personal history? When pressed for details, afterlife faith has issues.

These very practical considerations were not addressed in the Bible except by the Sadducees. They tried a little tricky casuistry on Jesus. They presented the hypothetical case of a woman who fell in with a seriously unhealthy family of seven brothers. As each died, she married the next until she had run out of prospects in the family. Seven brothers; seven funerals. Then she died. The Sadducees moved in for the kill, asking Jesus: "At the resurrection, then, whose wife will she be, for they had all married her?" Jesus was an artful dodger on this one. On the spot he came up with a sexless afterlife; there is no sex or marrying in heaven; all will be like angels (Matt. 22:23–30). Some of Jesus' highly sexed listeners might have wondered why the joy of sex was to be banned in the heavenly Paradise, and why they would still call it Paradise.

Interestingly, and showing that the gospels did not eschew spin, Matthew, after telling this story of Jesus and the mocking Sadducees, insists that Jesus had "silenced the Sadducees" (22:34). One can suspect that the Sadducees were not at all silenced or impressed by Jesus who claimed bodily personal resurrection that included sexual disembodiment. Jesus was in a fix. He could not say that polyandry was practiced in heaven, which is the only alternative to the woman's picking one of her former husbands and offending the other six. The only conclusion left to him was that sex had to go.

There are other problems when the dead do not stay put, problems with ramifications in domestic life. Matthew's Gospel says that when Jesus died, "there was an earthquake, the rocks split and the graves opened, and many of God's saints were raised from sleep; and coming out of their graves after his resurrection they entered the Holy City where many saw them" (Matt. 27:52). If among the "many" who saw the reborn dead were the widows or widowers of those people who had remarried after the death, it would be disconcerting. Would the resurrection of the dead spouses constitute a divorce, canceling out the subsequent marriage? Or would the new marriages trump the old? Would the newly risen be singled and free to start dating again? And, we are free to wonder who would want to date them, given their spooky past. Perhaps they would just have to settle for dating one another—assuming that they got their sex drive back having just come from the realm where there was no sex or marrying (Matt. 22:22–30).

Clearly, when death is no longer definitive, dicey problems abound. During his own lifetime, Jesus is said to have raised some dead to life. There was the young man in Nain, the daughter of Jairus, a synagogue-ruler, and Jesus' friend Lazarus. A. N. Wilson wonders about all these formerly dead: "Did they, like Jesus, ascend into heaven, or did they have their dying to do over again."[13] One sees the wisdom in the old saying: "Let the dead lie."

But no, the dead were not to be allowed to "rest in peace." Irenaeus, an important Christian leader in provincial Gaul in the second century, boasted: "We even raise the dead, many of whom are still alive among us, and completely healthy."[14] (A nightmare for probate lawyers.) The fact that they arose "completely healthy" implies that they were hormonally healthy and no longer sexless—giving resurrection something of a Cialis/Viagra effect.

After wading through all these conundrums the fresh air of good sense can be welcomed in the words of Bible scholar John Dominic Crossan: "I do not think that anyone, anywhere, at any time brings dead people back to life."[15] Amen! Refreshing, too, is Thomas Cahill's observation on the promises at Sinai: "Long life is promised to those who take care of their parents, but *eternal* life is promised to no one. No one had even thought of such a thing."[16]

Paul's Bottom Line

Paul was an excellent salesman for the aborning new religion he was helping to shape. He really put all his eggs in the afterlife basket, a perquisite that competing religions did not offer—or at least did not offer with comparable clarity. This gave him a competitive edge. Jesus' resurrection was paradigmatic for the resurrection of all. So, if it didn't happen to Jesus, it would not happen to anyone. "If there be no resurrection, then Christ was not raised; and if Christ was not raised, then our gospel is null and void, and so is your faith" (1 Cor. 15:13–14). But Paul was dead sure that Jesus did not stay dead.

In Christ Jesus, he said, death was vanquished. Paul could stand above death and mock it. "Our mortality has been clothed with immortality. . . . Death is swallowed up; victory is won! O Death, where is your victory? O Death, where is your sting? . . . God be praised, he gives us the victory through our Lord Jesus Christ" (1 Cor. 15:54–57). Alas, after all this bombast, poor Paul died and has not been heard from since. (And yet, though he did not escape the sting of death, his writings did.)

Paul—who focused more on the defeat of death than Jesus did—and who had more influence on what Christianity became than Jesus did—had hit on humanity's deepest dread, and he was selling a cure for it. "Fear," said the ancient Lucretius, "was the first mother of the gods . . . fear, above all, of death."[17] Ernest Becker centered on this natural human fear: "Anxiety is the result of the perception of the truth of one's condition. What does it mean to be a self-conscious animal? . . . It means to know that one is food for worms. This is the terror: to have emerged from nothing, to have a name, consciousness of self, deep inner feelings, an excruciating inner yearning for life and self-expression—and with all this yet to die."[18] It is said that animals experience death as something that happens to another. What Leonard Shlain calls "the Paleolithic epiphany" is the discovery that our parents and we ourselves will die. This epiphany is pan-human. Children, usually around seven, he says, come to awareness that they and their parents are mortal.

Historically, "once the implications of this dark thought sank in, a disquieting anxiety began to gnaw." To counter death's "crushing finality, humans conceived of an afterlife." As the body decayed, they conceived of "the self as an ectoplasmic soul capable of leaving the visible world to live on. . . . Archeologists have excavated reverential burials dating back sixty thousand years, and funerary rites became a defining characteristic among all human cultures."[19]

Religion is always an adventure into human psychology, and Paul was a virtuoso in reaching into human experience and feeling. Paul was immersed in Greek culture and that gave him distance from the problems posed by the Jewish sense of our essential bodiliness. In 1 Corinthians 15, he resorted to an oxymoron; the body of the resurrected person will be a "spiritual body." This body is not "from the dust of the earth," it is, rather, "from heaven." In our present state we die but there will be no dying when we get heaven-ized, when we "wear the likeness of the heavenly man" (vv. 45–49). So forget all about your nose job problem and dead spouses rising; forget your gender, too. Those are "flesh and blood" problems but "flesh and blood can never possess the kingdom of God" nor can "the perishable possess immortality" (v. 50).

The Montanists, who survived into the fifth century, claimed visions of what future life would be like. Gender differences seemed to disappear. In some visions they saw Jesus in female form.[20] Spiritual bodies could do sex change.

This spiritualizing of the body was tidy, but tidiness is not the hallmark of deep truths. The oxymoronic tidiness swept away all of the problems that come from embodiment. It didn't just move the goal posts; it tore them down and removed them and with them all the complications that arise from resurrecting the dead in bodily form.

Elsewhere on afterlife talk, Paul was not so tidy. Like many a salesman, he overpromised. That brings us to Paul's bungling in his letter to the Thessalonians.

Lost in the Clouds

Afterlife was big in the early Jesus movement even though it was not an obsession with Jesus from the little data we have. The oldest document in the Christian scriptures, Paul's first letter to the people of Thessalonika in Macedonia, was centered on surviving death. The epistle appeared around the year 50 CE, about twenty years after Jesus' death. Paul rehearsed his belief: "We believe that Jesus died and rose again; and so it will be for those who died as Christians; God will bring them to life with Jesus" (1 Thess. 4:14). Problem. Originally the Thessalonians were told that this would happen quickly while Paul's listeners were still alive. However, some of those who believed all that upped and died, and missed the big return. What about them?

Paul met the problem head on. He came up with a scenario that would take care of everyone, the dead and the quick, and he said he had this straight from the Lord:

> For this we tell you as the Lord's word: we who are left alive until the Lord comes shall not forestall those who have died; because at the word of command, at the sound of the archangel's voice and God's trumpet call, the Lord himself will descend from heaven; first the Christian dead will rise, then we who are left alive shall join them, caught up in clouds to meet the Lord in the air. (1 Thess. 4:15–18)

That was quite a scene that Paul orchestrated. Unfortunately, for Paul, not a single thing he predicted ever happened.[21] (As mentioned earlier, the Lord himself was way off base on this, too, unless Mark cribbed it from Paul and attributed the words to Jesus. Mark says that when Jesus spoke of the day of glory he said: "I tell you this: the present generation will live to see it all" [Mark 13:24–30].)

As blundered predictions go, this was a whopper. This is the oldest treatment of afterlife in the Christian scriptures, written some twenty years before the first gospel and it was wrong in all of its details. Things were promised that would be witnessed by those to whom Paul wrote. And those things never happened. Jesus says: "I tell you this: there are some of those standing here who will not taste death before they have seen the kingdom of God already come in power" (Mark 8:38, 9:1). Jesus also talked, according to Mark, of the clouds as the locus of this big sky event.

Paul's afterlife predictions were a muddle. At one time he states that no one is united with Jesus in the clouds or anywhere else until Jesus makes his dramatic return. But elsewhere, writing to the Philippians and the Corinthians, Paul says those who die are "with Christ." No waiting period (Phil. 1:23; 2 Cor. 5:8). When it comes to Paul's afterlife theories, more than Jesus is "up in the air."

Embarrassed by the Bible's indecision on all of this, later theologians joined the dissonant medley and proposed two postmortem judgments, *particular judgment* at the moment of death and *general judgment* at the time of the resurrection of all the dead.[22] This would eliminate the long wait in some holding area where the damned and the blessed would have to find some way of getting along. But, this solution does get sticky. The particular judgment would solve the waiting room problem, but why then would there be a need for a "general judgment" if the verdict was already delivered and acted on? It would be double jeopardy if a reversal were possible.

Rapture

With all these manifest errors and confusions, starting right in the Bible, one would think that modern Christians would shy from such texts. Not the Christian Right and fundamentalists. They ignore the embarrassment and run with the docking-in-space theory. In their terms it is the "rapture" (from the Latin *rapere*, to seize or take away). According to rapture mythology drawn right from those failed biblical texts, the end of the world is coming, and like Paul and Jesus, they think it imminent, and when it happens the good will be raptured from this planet up to meet Jesus—where else but "in the clouds."

Since imagination is king in all of this, they add details that would be jaw-dropping surprises for Paul and Jesus. In his best seller, *The Late Great Planet Earth*, Hal Lindsey says that on the day of the Lord, when the Christians have been safely raptured into the clouds, God will then reveal himself in a special way to 144,000 Jews who are going to convert to belief in Jesus. These enthusiastic converts will embark on a period of intense evangelism, the likes of which the earth has never known. Lindsey is rhapsodic about this. Imagine, he says, "144,000 Jewish Billy Grahams turned loose on this earth."[23] It is an exciting prospect.

Heaven Here, Not Heaven Above

However—and this is huge—the great event starting in the clouds comes quickly down to earth in the Bible and does not move the drama to an otherworldly heaven. The Kingdom of God that was central to Jesus' preaching will unfold on this earth. It is this-worldly, not otherworldly. Matthew talks of angels coming from heaven to cleanse the earth of evil-doers so that the good can enjoy a paradise right here on earth (Matt. 13:36–43). The book of Revelation says those who kept faith would rise from their graves to reign on earth "with Christ for a thousand years," though the rest of the dead would "not come to life until the thousand years were over" (Rev. 20:4–8). So we see here lots of talk about the dead rising, but not to live in a parallel world called heaven. It is a vision of afterlife here on this earth, not afterlife in an alternate invisible universe called heaven.[24]

As J. Edward Wright puts it in *The Early History of Heaven*: "Rather than transport the righteous into the heavenly realm to be with God, the author of the Book of Revelation suggests that God will renew the entire cosmos and make the earth an Edenic paradise once again. The Christian hope of being ever with God will be realized not in heaven but on the 'new earth.'"[25] The Islamic heaven is very earthy, and, indeed, sexy. "Pious Muslims learn that luxurious palaces, verdant gardens, magnificent feasts, and all manner of unending pleasure await them as rewards for their fidelity to the ways of Islam."[26]

How to Go to Hell

Not all the dead are grateful. Some go straight to hell.

In the Christian scriptures, the opposite of Paradise, heaven, is Gehenna, the area of the afterlife reserved for unrepentant sinners. The root of the word shows it as a poetic symbol, a metaphor and not a place. Gehenna derives from "the valley of Hinnom" near Jerusalem. The area was stigmatized by the fact that child-sacrifice had been offered to Moloch there. At a later time it seems to have become the city dump, where rubbish was burned. It served as a symbol of punishment. It was obviously employed as negative reinforcement of moral norms. It was associated with "unquenchable fire" (Mark 9:43) or "eternal fire" (Matt. 18:8) or the place where the wicked are "cast into the furnace of fire" (Matt. 13:42, 50). As mentioned earlier, Mt. Etna was thought to be the entrance into hell in early medieval Christianity.

Hell was used to convey symbolically the idea that missing out on the moral vision of the Kingdom of God preached by Jesus and the other prophets was a disaster; in persuasive rhetoric it could be compared to consignment to the smoldering fires of the city dump, Gehenna. The idea of eternal punishment is not accepted by modern Christian theology for obvious reasons. It negates the favored idea of a merciful deity. The idea of a god who wants you to love him with your whole heart, your whole soul, and your whole mind but who will fry you for all eternity if you don't is not palatable. The idea of Purgatory gradually emerged to mitigate the scandal of hell. It meant that postmortem punishment could be temporary. It grew up gradually in Christianity but was not formally adopted by the Catholic Church until the Council of Lyons (1274) and the Council of Florence (1439).

Prior to that time, there was considerable confusion among the great teachers of Christianity. Augustine had sensed a need for some purifying place for those who were guilty of minor offenses but he wasn't sure about it. He argued tentatively that "there were some whose lives, though not perfect, had been good enough to deserve that they should be purified by fire . . . *per ignem quendam*." A mixed blessing to be sure. He said he would not assert it outright and dogmatically but concludes with some telling modesty: "I will not deny it; it may be true (*non redarguo, quia forsitan verum est*)." As Nineham puts it: "it is clear that such ideas were by no means central to [Augustine's] own thinking," meaning that Augustine did not share the dogmatic conviction of later conciliar orthodoxy. He was an agnostic on the issue.[27]

The very hedged teaching on the fate of the sinful and the not terribly sinful is presented in remarkably tentative terms by other writers also. The hedged language is revealing. Writers say of afterlife conditions: "It is not incredible that . . . ," "It may be, as some suggest . . . ," "This has led some to the opinion that. . . ."[28] How refreshing and better it would have been if they all had said, "actually we don't have any idea of what we are talking about." That would have the merit of candor.

Afterlife belief was so solidly ensconced in the Christian movement that a custom arose of having banquets and inviting the dead. Sometimes the believers would light a candle to represent them. These were joyous occasions—the people utterly confident that the dead were right there enjoying themselves. They tended to get a bit too convivial and raucous, and some abstemious bishops frowned on their excesses.

It was also believed that dreams about the dead were actual visitations of the dead and were thus further proof that the dead do live on. Augustine doubted this, but his argument was rather personal. He argued that this could not be true since his mother never visited him in his dreams and surely she would want to stop by now and then to see him. Nakashima Brock and Parker offer a wry comment on why neurotic old Augustine was not visited by his mom: "Actually, there may have been many in addition to Monica who would prefer to never see Augustine again, alive or dead."[29]

Fire wasn't the only torture in store for the dead. Some opined that purgatorial suffering might include subjection to extremes of heat and cold alternatively. This punitive torture would be of "the severest sort—far worse than anything that could be experienced in this world."[30] The opinion grew up among the concerned bereaved survivors that if the living prayed for the souls in Purgatory, the time served by those souls might be shortened. Masses still said for the dead are an enduring echo of this belief.

Limbo, more properly thought of as a dance, never made it into Catholic dogma and was even criticized by the conservative Pope Benedict XVI. It was principally the place for unbaptized babies who could not be admitted to heaven lacking as they did the baptismal passport. Thomas Aquinas assured us that these babies could have full natural happiness but not supernatural happiness, whatever that might mean. The dour St. Augustine, however, said these babies lacking baptism were in original sin and therefore would suffer a *poena levis*, a slight degree of positive punishment. Even if that *peona levis* were an eternal itch, it would be unspeakably cruel to inflict it on babies who never sinned and lacked baptism through no fault of their own.

Afterlife picturings are free-wheeling projections of life on earth. As Nineham puts it regarding medieval images of afterlife: "The heaven and hell of the mediaeval imagination are really extrapolations of this world; heaven is envisaged as a hierarchically ordered community comparable to the Frankish kingdom; the saints gathered before God are like the members of an earthly court surrounding their king, and the heavenly choir is modeled on a monastic choir singing the office before the high altar."[31]

Jiggledeegreen

The multiple fictions on afterlife should not be monopolized by learned scribes and seers. The people, too, can imagine. Some years ago, in the little town of Glenties, in County Donegal in Ireland, the pastor Fr. Arthur McCloone, told me of the afterlife imagined by one of his parishioners. She was a pious woman who firmly believed that death is not an end but a new beginning. However, she found all the postmortem fantasies contained in Catholic orthodoxy wanting. She found hell, purgatory, and even heaven as offered by the hierarchy unattractive, and she rejected them outright. She informed the local clergy (who wisely did not contradict her) that when we die we enter, one and all, into a place called Jiggledeegreen. Jiggledeegreen is a happy place. There is food and drink aplenty, good music and dancing (Irish dancing), and storytellers galore to entertain young and old. Tea is always at the ready and a wee drop of whiskey is there for the asking. Even the bad become good there in this welcoming jolly ambience. No purgatorial or hell fires are needed to chasten or punish bad folks. Baptism in mirth works as the cure for all moral ills. And every evening in Jiggledeegreen, angels join humans and together they laugh and sing the night away.

If monks can envision afterlife in terms monastic and royals can fashion it in the image of their pompous courts, then the lady from Glenties can stand among them with equal claim to orthodoxy and invite the whole gloomy lot of them to join her in the eternal rollicking sweetness of Jiggledeegreen.

Afterlife as Metaphor and Apartheid

When we reach the limits of facile knowing we turn to metaphor and symbol and there we expand our cognitive range. Metaphor allows us to reach up and through and beyond the clouds so that we can touch that which we cannot see. And that is well and good and the glory of poetry, as long as our reality contact is not lost. We'd best stay linked to the empirical order where our feet are planted as we think and imagine and symbolize and live out the drama and expansive play of poetry. Death presents huge challenges to the human mind and we naturally turn to metaphor. Our heaven and our hell *stand for*, are metaphors for, what we wish for our departed. We want the dead child to be happy and so we imagine a heavenly bliss for them. The Japanese Buddhists show metaphor in action when they imagine the lost fetus being welcomed into the arms of the godly Jizo where joy and fun await. The Temple of Jizo on the Mountain of the Purple Cloud, near Tokyo, is a kind of memorial park to commemorate aborted fetuses or dead infants. Images of Jizo, a figure who is thought to have loved playing with children, are everywhere along with toys and pinwheels. There is a small playground in the middle of the cemetery where children can be seen playing merrily. The mood is far from lugubrious. It is certainly not Augustine's

Limbo but it is also not a Jiggledeegreen for dead babies. There is a sense of the sadness of separation and yet a conviction that visiting and festooning the site brings joy to the departed babies.[32]

The death of children was commonplace in most of human history and is still so in impoverished arts of the world. My father was one of thirteen children born in his family in nineteenth-century Donegal and only five survived to adulthood. There was a saying that it was a poor family that did not have little angels in heaven praying for them. These little angels were the children who died of infections that could not be handled by the health care of the day. And so, again, metaphor was their refuge; it gave relief from the terrible pain of loss.

Since not all afterlife fates are the same because of the reward/punishment motif, the metaphor of hell is the brutal fate of the unrepentant sinner. Through this metaphor we wish hellish punishment for mass murderers and despots. We want vindication for the sufferings inflicted on us, sufferings that we have no power to resist in this life, and so we turn to metaphor to have the suffering delivered on them after their death. The metaphoric nature of the hell idea is visible in common parlance when we direct some malefactors or annoying people to go there right now.

Modern Agnosticism, Implicit and Explicit

In our secular society, even among the religious people living in a secular society, afterlife metaphors may be more rhetoric than belief. Anne Wilson Schaef, a psychotherapist, says that women tend to "realize that immortality is not a genuine possibility and spend little or no time worrying about it."[33] Charlotte Perkins Gilman suggested that death, for men, is the pivotal experience given their hunting and warring past, but for women it is birth. As a result she argues, men have a greater need for immortality, "a posthumous egoism, a demand for an eternal extension of personality" that amounts to "a limitless individualism."[34] There is not only individualism in afterlife fantasies; there is also an arrogant species-ism, a pretentious claim setting us above and apart from the rest of nature. It is the quintessential apartheid. As I wrote elsewhere:

> Afterlife might do more than opiate the social conscience with hope for the sweet by and by. It can make our earth-life the prologue, not the text and context of our being. It can deterrestrialize our identity . . . making us strangers in this paradise. . . . Estrangement is the gateway to enmity. If we have a claim on an afterlife, and the plants and the animals do not, we are not their kith and kin, nor do we share their perils. Earth as *prolegomenon* and earth as *destiny* are the ultimate in divergent worldviews and divergent ethics.[35]

The hubris of immortality also offers immunity from cosmic fate. When our solar star reaches the "red star" end of its days and earth with all of its contents is returned to its primeval stardust, the supposed immortals can look on from their zone of imagined otherness-of-being and watch the cataclysmic show. If they are damned and in hell they might not be allowed to peek.

Immortality and the Evolution of Species

Evolution poses questions for afterlife believers. The hardest question is: *when in the evolutionary process did immortality kick in?* Our divergence from the apes began about seven million years ago.[36] How far did evolution have to advance before we became immortal?

Homo erectus, 1.7 million years ago, was close to modern humans in body size, but the brain size was barely half of ours. Did brain size have to reach some critical mass and critical efficiency before we became immortal? *Homo neanderthalensis* appeared in Europe and Western Asia between 130,000 and 40,000 years ago. Some think it a separate species from *homo sapiens*, a title we have somewhat prematurely awarded ourselves. However, the Neanderthals had brains slightly larger than ours. They did some primitive toolmaking and they were the first humans to leave behind evidence of burying their dead and caring for their sick, signs of love and compassion that could be called *spiritual*. Might they have made the cut and become immortal? If they did evolve into immortality, and if they were a different species would we have to coexist with them in heaven or hell or wherever, or would they have a Neanderthal heaven where they could be with their own?[37] Would Jesus' sacrifice on the cross atone for their misdeeds?

Fifty thousand years ago complex tools and even jewelry appeared, signaling what Jared Diamond calls "The Great Leap Forward." Then around 40,000 years ago the Cro-Magnons arrived. At this point, Diamond says, "we are dealing with biologically and behaviorally modern humans."[38] They displayed real skills in making harpoons, spear-throwers, bows and arrows. Their carefully buried skeletons show genuine aesthetic and spiritual development. Afterlife-ists would probably confer immortality at this point. There is new evidence that humans do carry some Neanderthal genes. Some mating did occur. If Neanderthals could not look forward to eternal life, would humans who now carry some of their genes see their afterlife hopes diminished?

If you take the truth out to lunch, you can have a lovely afternoon. If you take out a fancy that trips over its lack of verisimilitude, embarrassment and indigestion await you. The questions in this chapter are embarrassing, but they are the natural children of the immortality hypothesis.

PART IV

THE QUEST FOR A GLOBAL ETHIC

CHAPTER 9

WHEN WE ARE AS REMOTE AS CHARLEMAGNE

This is an eerie moment in human history, a moment when fear might be humanity's greatest need. Fear has big eyes, according to an old proverb. It is also a cure for distraction. We are so ominously distracted that it could signal that we are a failed species, destined for a short stay (in cosmic time) in this privileged corner of the universe. We can only look at the sun for an instant, and then we look away. We similarly shrink from the disasters we are setting in place, so the need is to "look at the sun" and then commence an epochal ethical pause to go searching for the ingredients of a global ethic that just might give us grounds for realistic hope.

Theistic religions have not distinguished themselves at this time of planetary peril. They have taken Hamlet too seriously: "There's a divinity that shapes our ends, rough hew them how we will." That's the "let God do it" copout. Meanwhile it is precisely our rough-hewing that is subverting nature and there is no divinity out there to reshape our ways. Forget Hamlet; listen to Gandhi. "As human beings our greatness lies not so much in being able to remake the world—that is the myth of the Atomic Age—as in being able to remake ourselves."[1] It is past time to look at any insights into our weird but magnificent species whether those insights come from science, social science, philosophy, or, yes, even religion. As for religions, forget their deity and afterlife creations, and recognize that they are at root poetry-rich philosophies that have hit on things that are stunningly relevant, with no authority behind them other than good sense.

The Sky Is Falling

Scientists and social scientists have superseded religious zealots in apocalyptic warnings. In his book *Collapse: How Societies Choose to Fail or Succeed*, Jared Diamond points out that all societies face ups and downs, but some of them absolutely and totally collapse, leaving behind monumental ruins that we visit as tourists. We marvel at the scale of these wondrous ruins, and try to imagine the wealth and power that built them. Still, as Diamond says: "Lurking behind this romantic mystery is the nagging thought: might such a fate eventually befall our own wealthy society? Will tourists someday stare mystified at the rusting hulks of New York's skyscrapers much as we stare today at the jungle-overgrown ruins of Mayan cities?"[2]

The oceans grow heftier by the day, fed by waters from melting glaciers and ice caps. Hurricane Sandy in 2012 was one more canary dropping. Offended nature is striking back at us. It can scorch as well as inundate. An article in the *Proceedings of the National Academy of Sciences* linked the record-breaking heat wave that hit Moscow in 2010 with global warming. So, too, the deadly European heat wave in 2003 and droughts like the one in Oklahoma and Texas in 2011.[3]

What is at once encouraging and discouraging is that the causes of this have been analyzed and *we may still have time to set reversals in motion*. Archaeologists, climatologists, historians, and paleontologists spell out the eight ways in which societies undermined themselves: by wrecking their *oikos*: *deforestation and habitat destruction, soil erosion and salinization, water management problems, overhunting, overfishing, foreign species affecting native species, human population growth, and increased per capita impact of people.*[4] If you want to devastate planetary life, that's the script to follow and we are following it to the letter like simple-minded disciples of doom.

Science has mapped out the road to hell and we, in an epic of distractedness with only intermittent corrective wiggles and tentative nods toward sanity, are plowing ahead on that road to hell, ignoring all the Bridge Out Ahead signs.

In 2009 I was invited to participate in a debate on abortion at University College, Dublin. I opened by scolding my Irish audience. "You have packed the house tonight to discuss abortion. If you want to be pro-life try to remember that you are an island nation, with few highlands, and the oceans are coming." My scold was ignored and we got right down to the current Catholic obsession with pelvic zone issues, fiddling with sex while the oceans swell and choke on our poisons.

Edward O. Wilson wonders, "How we will be remembered a thousand years from now when we are as remote as Charlemagne?"[5] Carl Sagan also looks a thousand years ahead but he is sure that at that time "historians, if there are any, will look back on our time as being . . . a turning point, a branch point in human history." If we survive, "this time will be remembered as the time when we could have destroyed ourselves and came to our senses and did not." With even more sureness he says that in a thousand years or even a million years, the Earth will be here. "The question, the key question, the central question—in a certain sense, the only question—is, will we?"[6]

The answer is: If current trends continue, we will not.

With a kind of chilling calmness, Swedish scientist George Henrik von Wright says: "One perspective, which I do not find unrealistic, is of humanity as approaching its extinction as a zoological species. The idea has often disturbed people. . . . For my part I cannot find it especially disturbing. Humanity as a species will at some time with certainty cease to exist; whether it happens after hundreds of thousands of years or after a few centuries is trifling in the cosmic perspective. When one considers how many species humans have made an end of, then such a natural nemesis can perhaps seem justified."[7]

Other dismal choristers join in this fearsome *pathetique*. Vaclav Havel warns that the battered earth might dispense with us in the interest of a higher value, that is, life itself. Biologist Lynn Margulis observes that the rest of earth's life did very well without us in the past and it will do very well without us in the future. And New York

University physics professor Marty Hoffert adds: "It may be that we are not going to solve global warming, the earth is going to become an ecological disaster, and somebody will visit in a few hundred million years and find there were some intelligent beings who lived here for a while, but they just could not handle the transition from being hunter-gatherers to high technology. It's entirely possible."[8]

Too Many People, Too Little Earth

Of the eight causes leading to societal collapse overpopulation is prime. A formula might sum it up: H + A + A = A: *Hyperfertility* + *Affluence* + *Appetite* = *Apocalypse.* Affluence breeds appetite. Increasing numbers plus growing appetite crashes apocalyptically against the earth's limits. Biologist Harold F. Dorn says with elemental logic: "No species has ever been able to multiply without limit. There are two biological checks upon a rapid increase in numbers—a high mortality and a low fertility. Unlike other biological organisms [humans] can choose which of these checks shall be applied, but one of them must be."[9] Nature is already applying this stern law. Some forty million people die every year from hunger and poverty-related causes—the equivalent of three hundred jumbo jet crashes daily, with half of the passengers being children.[10] Twenty-five thousand people die every day from drinking contaminated water. "Official estimates suggest that 70 percent of India's water is polluted and forty-one of the forty-four largest cities in China have polluted groundwater."[11] It has been said that if one glass of clean water were a cure for AIDS most of the world's people would have no access to it.

A further frightening statistic: half the world's residents are under 25; there are one billion adolescents. The reproductive behavior of the young is unpredictable. Young men have sperm that can leap over tall buildings in a single bound and we do not know what these young fertiles will do. Hence, the future estimate of human numbers vary, peaking at nine, ten, or eleven billion people on a planet where no more than three billion of us could live and consume as the affluent do.[12]

Conservatives as Worshippers of Dead Liberals

Thomas Aquinas is the super-saint when it comes to Catholic theology. At the Council of Trent in the sixteenth century, two books were placed on the altar: the Bible and the *Summa Theologiae* of Thomas Aquinas. Therefore, it is surprising and little noted that Thomas saw the need for birth control and even said it should be enforced by law if need be. Ironically, Thomas is the hero of conservative Catholics who have not read his works.

Commenting on Aristotle's *Second Book of Politics*, Thomas agreed with Aristotle that excessive population growth would promote poverty, conflict, and social chaos as demand exceeds resources. Population must not be permitted to grow beyond a determined number. As Catholic author Johannes Messner comments in his *magnum opus* on natural law, Thomas insists that we cannot have peace and equity in our society "and at the same time allow an infinite growth of the population."[13] Thomas does not get into the thorny issues of just how a just state will manage this fertility limitation but he stands with Aristotle in seeing its necessity. He does break with Aristotle when Aristotle speaks of the idea of encouraging men to have sex with men to avoid generation of children. Thomas condemns this "*turpem masculorum coitum*" (*Lectio* 15), but he does not condemn the need for population management.

The Infinity Lies

The hard fact that did not penetrate into classical economics is that the resources of earth are finite. Growth, therefore, cannot be infinite. Neither can waste. The earth is a closed system and nothing gets out. Unless we start shipping our waste into space, it's piling up here polluting land and sea. But the infinity illusion has deep roots. Starting in the eighteenth century exuberant optimism became the prevailing myth. This was a major shift. Ancient writers such as Xenophon, Hesiod, and Empedocles believed that human society was decaying away from the "golden age" of yesteryear. Pessimism was king. The idea of a lost *aetas aurea* shows up in societies as diverse as China and the Cherokee Indians. But as science got smart, we got cocky and high on infinity illusions. A new myth toppled the old.

It is a rule of life that as we demythologize, we remythologize.

In the new myth, progress, not decay, is our destiny. This juvenile optimism found influential expression in the Bretton Woods agreement of July 1944. In the opening session, Henry Morgenthau, the U.S. Secretary of the Treasury and president of the conference, read a welcoming message from President Roosevelt. He set the fatal tone of the gathering. He predicted the "creation of a dynamic world economy in which the people of every nation will be able to realize their potentialities in peace and enjoy increasingly the fruits of material progress on an earth *infinitely* blessed with natural resources"(emphasis added).[14] This was the group that was fashioning the World Bank and the International Monetary Fund, and laying the groundwork for the General Agreement on Tariffs and Trades, that is, the foundations of the postwar world. And it was their faith "that prosperity has no fixed limits. It is not a finite substance to be diminished by division." This is fictive dogma, a feat of transubstantiation hocus-pocus where the finite is pronounced infinite.

This oxymoronic and moronic dogma of infinite growth on a finite earth became the ruling assumption in the mythology of economics. Environmental concerns became "externalities," a put-down if ever there was one. This ignores the fact, as Al Gore said, that the economy is the wholly owned subsidiary of the environment. Those meeting at Bretton Woods were not cold-hearted schemers. They hoped to end poverty and its resultant chaos, but their panacea was growth. Growth is the new divinity that shapes our ways. It is a new kind of fundamentalism. Instead of "let God do it" this is "let growth do it." Corporations became the high priests of growth. (In the U.S. Supreme Court's *Citizens United* these entities were elevated to personal status—demigods, actually.) The result of this modern apotheosis is what David Korten calls "a global financial system that has become the world's most powerful governance institution." National governments are demoted to minions, liege to the market. And this newly created "governance institution" is not "of the people, for the people, by the people," much less for the environment.[15]

The Gods Do Not Die from Denial, They Resurface

Homo sacralis (aka *homo sapiens*) will not be without gods. Religion is a response to the sacred and as one sacred is removed another steps in. As mentioned earlier, Buddhist philosopher David R. Loy says that the capitalist market is functioning like a religion, issuing its commandments from its own Olympus and its own Sinai, superseding the increasingly dysfunctional major religious traditions. God used to be seen as *disponens omnia fortiter* and *suaviter*, managing everything with sweet gentleness and strength. Such a god merited absolute trust. With this god deposed, the Market ascends the throne *fortiter et suaviter disponens omnia.* The market religion is booming binding all corners of the globe into a worldview and set of values that we think secular but is functioning with religious fervor. Traditional religions, eat your hearts out; you have never matched the missionary zeal and success of this divine pretender.

The Kill-Power God

Here in Part IV of this book I argue that there are brilliant insights in the world's religions that secular minds tut-tuttingly eschew. But first let us join many secular minds in admitting the messes that religions have made and fomented. Not to be forgotten is the stinging and telling indictment leveled by Lynn White Jr. in his famous 1967 essay charging that Christianity "bears a huge burden of guilt" for the ecocrisis.[16] It helped to set us above—and thus against—the rest of nature. Jack Nelson-Pallmeyer points to another crucial sin of the major Western religions.

In his book *Is Religion Killing Us?* Nelson-Pallmeyer cites the "violence-of-God traditions that are the heart of the Bible and the Qur'an. This is the elephant in the room of which nobody speaks."[17] Both religious traditions promote the idea of power as *dominion over*, power as dominance and violence as salvific. The crusaders didn't have to make it up. It was there for the plucking. The error, however, is not isolated in the religions. As Nelson-Pallmeyer says, it is part of the unifying faith of most moderns, including atheists, Marxists, politicians, revolutionaries, counter-revolutionaries, communists, capitalists, anarchists, and government leaders who bankrupt their nations buying kill power. "If religion and faith are about ultimate allegiance, then it can be said that violence is the world's principal religion."[18]

Is It Too Late?

Ecocide is the fatal mission on which our species has carelessly embarked, employing only ineffectual *beaux gestes* to brake our momentum. The more hopeful scientists tell us that we have *a generation at most* to bring about a radical change in our production/consumption habits and our relationship to the earth. After that we will face a major tipping point, a "point of no return," when devastating changes will be beyond our capacity to reverse and will be irreversible.[19] *Worldwatch* magazine once headlined its editorial: "It May Not Be Too Late." That is as reassuring as a pilot announcing on takeoff, "This plane may not crash." What's worse—or better, if you have hope—scientists, unlike religious apocalyptics, talk numbers and even dates. John Bellamy Foster and Brett Clark offer dates on the falling of the sky: "The point of irreversible climate change is usually thought of as a 2 degree Centigrade (3.6 F) increase in global average temperature, which has been described as equivalent at the planetary level to the 'cutting down of the last palm tree' on Easter Island."[20] Climate scientists at Oxford University put this "planetary point of no return" at the year 2043 when cumulative carbon emissions may reach one trillion metric tons.[21]

As Foster and Clark point out, "climate science is not exact enough to pinpoint precisely how much warming will push us past a planetary tipping point. But all the recent indications are that if we want to avoid planetary disaster we need to stay considerably below 2 degrees Centigrade."[22] It is at that point, as climatologist James Hansen states, we face a "planetary emergency since we will have started a process that is out of humanity's control."[23]

That's the sun from whose glare we seek shade.

A Word of Hope, Please!

Thomas Kuhn spoke a word of hope that has echoed widely. In *The Structure of Scientific Revolution*, he argues that creativity rises in our species when we hit an impasse, a brick wall. It means that the prevailing paradigm is inadequate and a crack is opened for new models of thought. "Just as scientific revolutions are inaugurated by a growing sense that the existing paradigm has ceased to function adequately, political resolutions are inaugurated by a growing sense that the existing institutions have ceased adequately to meet the problems posed by an environment that they have in part created."[24]

Clifford Geertz also says that the quest for meaning, for doing serious rethinking, is sharpened when human limits are broached. When ultimate push comes to ultimate shove, we stretch. Crises after all did push the human brain to grow. Justice means giving what is due to people and to all of nature, and Geertz says we ultimately cannot bring ourselves to accept "that justice is a mirage. The instinct to meaning will not be denied."[25] Part of ethics involves choking. The hope is that our ethical choke reflex will happen when we face and experience the horrors we are wreaking. It could lead us to reject the cosmologies that the prevalent ethic underwrites and calls normal. The environmental doomsday date listed earlier is beginning to trigger the ethical choke reflex. The old normal must be buried. When Chris Hedges reminds us that more than two million children were killed in wars during the 1990s, and that three times that number were disabled or seriously injured, and that twenty million children were displaced from their homes in 2001 alone, that data is choking. There is something wrong with the operative paradigms. The possibility of changing them cannot be a mirage. Or so we hope.

The End of Military History

In an epic of hubris, Francis Fukuyama gained unaccountable fame for announcing "the end of history" and the definitive triumph of Western liberalism. (Preferable is Gandhi's caustic witticism: when asked what he thought of Western civilization, he replied, "That would be a wonderful idea.") With overdue realism Andrew Bacevich, a man with solid military credentials, wrote of "The End of Military History" and the failure of the Western way of war. Western military thinking rested on the belief in the "plausibility of victory." This faith—and it was faith—began to erode as early as World War I. It has now "disappeared altogether . . . among nations classified as liberal democracies." Only two nations resisted this trend, the United States and Israel. Both placed their security on "unambiguous military superiority." They have that superiority now, and neither nation is secure—and minds are changing slowly in both nations. Even General Petraeus admitted, "we can't kill our way out of" the fix we're in. Bacevich calls this statement "a eulogy on the Western conception of warfare of the last two centuries."[26]

The Greeks had two words for time: *chronos*, which is the time measured on clocks, and *kairos*, which signals opportune time, a moment when many possibilities converge. Ecologically, economically, and politically, the inundation of failures and the embarrassment of regnant paradigms might make this a *kairos* moment. Time to think new thoughts but also to salvage old wisdom—from every possible source—to save us from making history a repetition of errors and a cascade of disasters.

Wilson ends his book *The Future of Life* on a tentatively hopeful note. He criticized "the cynicism endemic to the conservative temperament." Our central problem he says, "is how to raise the poor to a decent standard of living worldwide while preserving as much of the rest of life as possible." He shares the conviction "of many thoughtful people from all walks of life, that the problem can be solved. Adequate resources exist. Those who control them have many reasons to achieve that goal, not least their own security. In the end, however, success or failure will come down to an ethical decision, one on which those now living will be defined and judged for all generations to come." Given our imaginative powers he concludes that we "will surely find the way to save the integrity of this planet and the magnificent life it harbors."[27]

I am not as hopeful as Edward O. Wilson but I am not devoid of hope. Otherwise I could not attempt what I shall now do, to look for important deposits of wisdom in sources where skittishly dogmatic secularists dare not tread. On those sources I shall attempt to break the secular sound barrier. The wisdom to be found in these sources is natural, not supernatural, born of experience and human genius and poetic literary power, and the contemporaneity of it is nothing less than stunning. To that task I now proceed.

CHAPTER 10

IS YOU IS OR IS YOU AIN'T MY BABY?

The scientist Jacob Bronowski confronted the ultimate question on the state and fate of humanity one night in 1945 when he was driven in a Jeep though the ashy ruins of Nagasaki. In the dark he could not even see if they had moved from the open country into the city since what was left of the city was a dark and desolate wasteland. The only sound he could hear was that of an American military radio playing the popular tune "Is You Is or Is You Ain't My Baby?" In the context, the question was piercingly relevant. What he saw was "civilization face to face with its own implications. The implications are both the industrial slum that Nagasaki was before it was bombed, and the ashy desolation that the bomb made of the slum. And civilization asks of both ruins, 'Is You Is or Is You Ain't My Baby?'"[1]

That question—phrased variously—has tugged at the human mind since we began our stumbling quest for truth. Arthur Schopenhauer says that "all philosophers in every age and land have blunted their wits on it."[2] It is, quite simply, the *moral* question. The moral question arises from the awed discovery that there is on the surface of the earth a delicate phenomenon, weight-wise almost nothing compared to the ponderous mass of the planet. This phenomenon is not only light, it is fragile. The name we give to it is *life*, and the quest to protect and enhance it is called *ethics*. Insects and animals are genetically inscribed to work for their common good. We're not. Ethics is what we have. Ethics is the effort to discern what is good for us and the rest of nature, and what is not. We have never been good at it and so Lenin was being none too cynical when he described human history as "a butcher's bench."

Ethics did have a privileged position in early American education. Take Amherst College, for example. Look at its bulletin from 1895. The whole first page was given over to a description of the course on ethics. It is given to seniors, taught by the president of the college, and is clearly intended to be the capstone of the educational process. The philosophy behind this was that students were not considered educated if their moral intelligence had not been refined by the study of ethics. As the Amherst College Catalogue put it: "The aim of the course is by the philosophic study of the social and political relations of the individual to his fellow citizens and to the State, to promote that moral thoughtfulness . . . which is the strongest element in true patriotism."[3] That's nice. To be patriotic is to be morally thoughtful. But, wait. Check out the college bulletin just ten years later, in 1905, and you discover that ethics has been demoted from the front page. At Amherst, it became an elective for sophomores; in many colleges it disappeared. As Douglas Sloan writes, this downgrading of the study of ethics was "emblematic of a major change that had overtaken the whole of American higher education."[4]

Since ethics is figuring out what is good for human life and all of life on this generous speck of the universe, dropping it or demoting it is no minor happening. What happened? What happened was infatuation. Science as savior displaced ethics. Indeed the stalwart purveyors of ethical theory, to try to get a hearing, had to market their product as "the science of ethics."[5] Science and ethics are not enemies. Indeed, science, to be human, must be wed to ethics and ethics must open its arms to the data of science. "Value-free" science is an illusion, an illusion we gag on as we breathe and as we walk or jog over ground waters filling with poison. Science has prepared the end of the world and stored it in our nuclear silos and weapons and in the hundreds of thousands of chemicals that roam untested in our midst. The can-do's of science must be civilized by the oughts of ethics. And, often, they have not been. History was split in two when the bombs dropped on Hiroshima and Nagasaki. Before then, nature's restorative powers were greater than our destructive power. On this side of the bomb, we upstarts can triumph over nature's healing ways.

Awakening from Moral Slumbers

Our downside is an old story. Humans, the first form of terrestrial life capable of thought, are ingenious enough to make awful messes. We are more clever than wise. Moses saw this and so he went up the mountain to try to get some moral norms carved in stone. The human race saw it after the two international blood baths in the first half of the twentieth century, and up the mountain the United Nations went in 1948, using the vernacular of human rights, not commandments, to bring moral intelligence to bear on our lethality. More recently insistent calls are heard for a "global ethic," one that would be fully sensitive to cultural diversities while reaching for the shared values rooted in the *humanum*. These calls for moral sanity are coming from the most unexpected sources with an unparalleled unanimity. Rip Van Winkle is awakening. And even religions, those symbolic powerhouses that often sideline themselves with their dogmatic extravagances, are downplaying their dogmas in deference to humanity's survival needs. Catastrophic prospects make strange bedfellows and maybe just in time.[6]

The Demise of National Sovereignty

The early American hunger for a *novus ordo saeclorum*, a new world order, has gone global. National sovereignty no longer works; it is political autism. As Jonathan Schell says, "sovereignty was first asserted in Europe by absolutist kings as a scythe to cut down the tangled thickets of medieval political institutions, with their dense, overlapping webs of ecclesiastical as well as secular rights, privileges and duties."[7] That was then; that is not now. Now, Schell says: "The need for global political structures to deal with the globalized economy and the swiftly deteriorating global environment is manifest."[8] But is it possible? Can nations, the modern tribes, surrender their independent sovereignty to enter into cooperative co-government?

As Schell notes, this is what actually happened in the Good Friday accord in Northern Ireland. "We will look in vain in this agreement for power that can be called sovereign. The people of Northern Ireland remain citizens of the United Kingdom, yet they have been granted a constitutional right that the citizens of few, if any other nation states enjoy—the right to remove themselves and their land and goods to another country upon a majority vote."[9]

The possible is now underway. The European Union, staggered but still standing, is historic. The former chancellor of Germany Helmut Schmidt said it "marks the first time in the history of humankind that nation-states that differ so much from each other nevertheless . . . have *voluntarily* decided to throw in their lot together."[10]

But, Mr. Schmidt, it is not the first time. The United Nations Charter, which should be read daily by heads of state who signed on to it, tolled the knell of sovereignty in the use of state sponsored violence, that is, war. As Richard Falk writes:

> World War II ended with the historic understanding that recourse to war between states could no longer be treated as a matter of national discretion, but must be regulated to the extent possible through rules administered by international institutions. The basic legal framework was embodied in the U.N. Charter, a multilateral treaty, largely crafted by American diplomats and legal advisors. Its essential feature was to entrust the Security council with administering a prohibition of recourse to international force (Article 2, Section 4) by states except in circumstances of self-defense, which itself was restricted to responses to prior 'armed attack' (Article 51), and only then until the Security Council had the chance to review the claim.[11]

Having helped craft this moral and political revolution at the United Nations, American leaders have since led the way in trashing it, but it did get into the Charter and it was something brand new under the sun.

Embarrassed into Peace?

Supplementing this new postsovereignty move toward cooperation and a new world order is the rise of military science. As we saw, Andrew Bacevich envisions the end of military history; overwhelming military superiority no longer translates into security. The bomb-makers deserve great credit. They have made it hard for any war to do more good than harm, a basic necessity for any moral action. Any actions that do more harm than good are properly called stupid as well as immoral. War outside of the policing paradigm enshrined in the U.N. Charter precludes all "winning." War outside of the policing paradigm born in the U.N. Charter has lost its claim to rationality or moral standing.

The doctrine of "deterrence" that reigned for decades amounted to a policy of "retaliatory genocide." Barbarity could not be made of nastier stuff. It is good news that kill-power has overreached itself. It has developed to the point where it flunks any cost/benefit test. According to the State Department, forty-four nations have the capacity to develop nuclear weapons, meaning that retaliatory genocide could become the coin of the international realm. Sensible fright may stem that. Very destabilizing is the fact that four nations, Israel, India, Pakistan, and Cuba, have refused to join the nonproliferation treaty. After their dealings with North Korea, Pakistan was described as "the K-Mart of nuclear weapons technology." At any rate, the doomsday technology is out there and getting legs.

How effective are nuclear weapons in international conflicts? Six nuclear-armed nations have lost wars to non-nuclear nations. How embarrassing! The United States, the superpower supreme, has a streak of four lost wars in a row: Korea, Vietnam, Iraq, and Afghanistan. Nothing the United States achieved in those places could credibly be called *victory*. Britain, Israel, the Soviet Union, China, and France found in their wars that nuclear weapons were of no more use than a bull in a china shop. There is a growing hunger for a revival of the art of diplomacy and mediation, but hands grown rough with bludgeoning are poor candidates for doing the needlepoint of diplomacy.

At this writing, there is only the dimmest perception abroad that war technology has turned this epochal corner. Burgeoning drone technology is a big part of that. When change in the technology of war happens, history shows that it takes a long time for the "duh" moment of recognition and readjustment to arrive. Barbara Ehrenreich, in her brilliant book *Blood Rites: Origins and History of the Passions of War*, shows how our species falls into rituals and rote even when it comes to slaughter. Going back to the fourteenth century we find that the Europeans had pretty much ritualized their modes of state-sponsored violence. Soldiers showed up in a field bedecked in armor and distinguishing colors so you could tell friend from foe. Knights in expensive armor were state of the art.

Locked into this framework, the French nobles arrived for battle at Crecy in 1346. Alas, the British had come upon the longbow and realized that they could train peasant longbowmen on the cheap and mow the French down from a safe distance. One would think that French military intelligence would take note of that. But no, ten years later at Poitier, "as if in a state of collective psychological denial," as Ehrenreich puts it, they once again rode to their death in a hail of arrows. Even as late as 1415 at Agincourt, the French only partially got the point.[12] After this it seems they turned to a teenage girl, Joan of Arc, to see if she could figure out the new modes of war. It constitutes a remarkable, but not atypical, chapter in the "war for dummies" archives.

We should spare the French our scorn for their doltish obtuseness. The United States arrived in Vietnam dressed and ready for World War II. It was the American Crecy moment. We then had our Poitier and Agincourt moments in Iraq and Afghanistan as guerilla warfare undid our outmoded tools of hyperpower.

And now the drones, the new longbow. Proliferation of this "killing by remote control" is going pell-mell. The technology supporting drones is stunning. Medea Benjamin writes: "With their astonishing sensors, from several miles in the air they can follow the route of a suspicious-looking pick-up truck or track a sniper on a rooftop. The Predator's infrared camera can even identify the heat signature of a human body form 10,000 feet in the air. From 8,000 miles away in

Nevada, a drone pilot can watch an Afghan as he lights up cigarettes, sits talking to friends on a park bench, or goes to the bathroom—never imagining that anyone is watching him."[13]

All this is in its technological infancy. Even now the Reaper can linger in the air for about eighteen hours. "In the future, high altitude UAVs using solar power—or powered by ground-based lasers, or using air-to-air refueling—will be able to remain airborne indefinitely."[14]

The Other Vatican

The need for transnational authority structures has been forcefully defended in a document coming out of the Vatican. Yes, the Vatican! There is more than one Vatican. There is the Vatican that stresses pelvic zone orthodoxy and they are noisy, intrusive, and well known. This part of the Vatican is in belated but still too slow decline. But there is another working on the neglected Catholic social justice tradition with roots in Judaism and early Christianity. Its work shows up in a 2011 document with the unwieldy but informative title: "Towards Reforming the International Financial and Monetary Systems in the Context of Global Political Authority." This emanates from Pope Benedict's Pontifical Council on Justice and Peace, and it caused apoplectic reactions from the Catholic right wing.

The document calls for globalized solutions for globalized problems; it favors a market economy but not this one; it calls for "supranational authority," a healthy, nontyrannical "world political authority" to tame the greed games that strip the poor and engorge the rich; it calls names. It derides "neoliberalism," the neoconservatives' credo, as devoid of "moral perspective" and a writ for "collective greed." (As Nicholas Fargnoli says, much that is called *capitalism* could best be called *greedalism*.) The Vatican document calls for taxation of financial transactions to create a "world reserve fund." It moves beyond the tribal assumptions of "Westphalian" nation-states and calls for a world community where differences would be respected and honored for a common good. It expands the idea of the "common good" to all nations and to all of nature. It is a gem of a document that shouldn't be ignored because of its birthplace.

Notice how morality and dogma can part company. Nothing in this thoughtful Vatican document requires a belief in a personal deity or postmortem life. The document accepts Deuteronomy's mandate "There shall be no poor among you!" (15:4) and Jesus' "good news for the poor" (Luke 4:18), as well as his scorching "woe to you rich" (Luke 6:24). But it doesn't require that you divinize Jesus or share Jesus' faith in a fatherly God.

More Radical Religion

In 1993 the Parliament of the World's Religions met in Chicago and issued a "Declaration Toward a Global Ethic." The document endorses the 1948 Universal Declaration of Human Rights of the United Nations. It condemns egoism, individual egoism, or collective egoism in the form of separatist nationalism. It says that both "totalitarian state socialism" and "unbridled capitalism have hollowed out and destroyed many ethical and spiritual values." It calls for the states to acknowledge "the authority of international organizations." This Parliament included representatives from almost all of the world's major and indigenous religions. And note again, it is, like the American constitution, a God-less document. It draws from the moral insights of the world's religions and presents them as relevant for "religious" and "nonreligious" persons, for theists and nontheists.

I stress this because many critics of religions feel you have to buy into the dogmatic assertions of religions to profit from any good sense or insights they may contain in their experience-fed moral philosophical memory. This is wrong to the point of dumb.[15]

Every creative thinker arrives with baggage from which they do not fully free themselves. As Buddhist scholar David Loy says, when the Buddha taught, he was immersed in a culture that believed in karma and rebirth. Some think this belief in multiple lives is essential to Buddhism. It is not, even if the Buddha accepted it.[16] The moral insights lodged in the Buddhist tradition remain embarrassingly relevant. Buddhism pointed to the key human failings of greed, delusion, and a lost sense of interdependency, a sense of how things connect and of how one thing leads to another. Subprime mortgages and derivatives would wither under the searing light of these ancient insights.

I have already cited earlier Erich Fromm's comments on Sigmund Freud's theoretical system. Fromm's observation has universal application. He cites the grip of cultural fixations on even original thinkers. Creative thought, whatever its illuminating discontinuities, is a captive to the thought and symbolic paths and patterns of one's culture. We carry baggage with us as we blaze new trails. Critique of the baggage can only come later, as is happening in Buddhism, Christianity, and elsewhere. Only then can old encumbrances be critiqued and shuffled off.[17]

The same insight can be applied to ancient thinkers from Plato, Aristotle, and Maimonides to Isaiah, Jesus, Paul, Mohammad, Lao-tzu, Confucius, and Gandhi. Creedal implants of myths such as reincarnation, afterlife, and personalized deities can be viewed critically and set aside as you probe the philosophy or poetry of the author. The underlying morality narrative of these epic probes into humanity does not stand or fall under the sway of transient myths. Hindu god-creation, for example, is irrepressible. If you take all of its theistic creations as literal entities their powerful poetic message is lost in the miasma of literalism.

Kairos

Kairos has been compared to a logjam. It is opportunity born of multiple inputs. Logs moving down river occasionally jam into a tight compaction. At that point you could walk across them. It doesn't last as logs are gradually dislodged and make their separate ways down the river, but while they cohere, things can happen. Many logs are jamming now. Threats are increasingly global, not local, as the environment breaks down and kill-power becomes uncontainable. Slaughter becomes less useful to achieve political ends. Economies interlock as corporations render national borders irrelevant and international finance crosses borders at light speed. Space travel changes perspectives since from space one can see no borders. The planet appears as one entity with one destiny. Religions, with all their symbolic clout, are uniting and sequestering their dogmatic constructions to focus on moral needs.

Once again, back to Gandhi's insight: as human beings, our challenge is not to just make stuff but "to remake ourselves."[18] "Where there is no vision, the people perish," said the ancients. We are poised to rethink our reality, and nature's stern and prodding sanctions are already knocking at the door. A new openness is born amid this remarkable confluence of chastening changes.

At this moment in history the bard is more important than the technician. Now, more than ever, the poet is a civil servant. To survive, a wobbling civilization mired in its prose must poetically expand. To that expansion we now attend, drawing on sources long neglected or buried in disdain.

CHAPTER 11

FROM PROSE TO POETRY

The Bible is called "the good book" and that's a mistake because some of it is awful, the gruesome record of barbaric times. All the evil "–ism's" find warranty there, from speciesism and militarism, to racism, sexism, heterosexism, and classism. A simple rubric from literary criticism rescues the book from misunderstanding and abuse: the key terms are *descriptive* and *prescriptive*. Much of the Bible is *descriptive* of the way life was lived in wild times and that is often disgusting. But there is also in that complex anthology a stream of poetry that rises to classical excellence. In its peak moments, the poetry of the Bible envisions, imagines, and *prescribes* whole new ways of restructuring human life. The poets (some of them called *prophets*) were conducting a workshop for a new humanity. In a modernity with diminished poetic sensibilities and *faux* sophistication, the *prescriptive* insights with their stunning applicability to modern plights are usually missed.[1] That, as Yeats could put it, is "a pity beyond all telling." And yet there is really no need to stumble over the muddle of biblical god-talk on the way to this classical morality epic.

Exodus/Sinai: History or Metaphor?

The Exodus/Sinai story in novels, films, and homilies suffers shrinkage; it gets reduced to historical facticity, that is, stuff that happened.

The Exodus may never have happened and Moses as an individual may never have existed. Like Yahweh, he may have been a composite of many personalities that were woven together with literary freedom. If you are writing factual narration this news might strike you as a loss, but if you are in the right literary genre, heroic poetry, your mind is being invited on safari into the realm of lost possibilities, possibilities that beckon still.

Bible readers long assumed that the drama of the Exodus was an historical event recorded by ancient journalists struggling to get their facts straight. Norman K. Gottwald throws cold water on this in his exhaustive study of the tribes of Yahweh. He refers to "the problematic historicity of the Exodus and our lack of much information about it."[2] Israel Finkelstein and Neil Asher Silberman are more blunt. Regarding the story of Moses leading the Hebrews out of bondage they write: "There was no mass Exodus from Egypt."[3] Robert Wright notes that "some biblical historians now doubt that Moses even existed, and virtually none now believe that the biblical accounts of Moses are reliable. These stories were written down centuries after the events they described" and were later edited by authors with an agenda to support their late developing monotheism and other interests.[4]

But this does not mean that nothing happened back there. Forget the frogs and parted seas engulfing the bad guys; what really happened was a dramatic revolution of political consciousness and social reorganization that the poetic authors were presenting in epic form. Feudalism and imperialism were the reigning paradigms of social organization and against enormous odds the tribes that became Israel took all of that on. For two remarkable centuries they had great success. It is not too much to say that they forced history to turn a corner and modern democratic theory stands in debt to their achievements.

Outlaws and Heretics

These Israelites, precociously literate at a time when writing was still young, were branded *apiru*, outlaws because they opposed the social organization of their neighbors. They were as threatening to their neighbors as the Sandinistas were to Ronald Reagan. They were political heretics with differences that often led to war but, as Gottwald says, "Israel broke totally free of feudalism and extended its 'outlaw' system over an entire region and an entire people, so that 'outlawry' became 'inlawry,' the basis of a new order. . . . In Israel we see an anti-feudal way of life which has become an entire counter-society."[5] Dynamic early Israel was a call "to a new form of social relations which destroys class privileges." The goal of this radical revolution was community presciently based on "egalitarian social relations." "Not only does Israel challenge Egyptian imperialism, it rejects city-state feudalism as well and does so by linking up exploited peoples across the boundaries of the old city-state divisions."[6]

The One Percent versus the Ninety-Nine Percent

This is more exciting than mythic tales of plagues sent upon the Pharaoh. This radical rethinking of social existence is more threatening to all Pharoahs, modern and ancient, than fictive plagues. It topples the mighty from their thrones. The Exodus/Sinai epic was people-power, the 99 percent taking on the 1 percent. It depended on a "consensual understanding of and commitment to common interests, requiring, as it were the ancient tribal equivalent of 'an enlightened and publicly active citizenry.'"[7] The 99 percent had to do it since the 1 percent was corrupt. The one percent were, as Micah put it, "rich men who are full of violence; the city's upper classes speak falsehood and their tongues frame deceit" (6:12).

Plus ça change, plus c'est la même chose. The ancient poets of Israel indicted this penchant of the hyper-rich for exploitative connivances and they did so millennia before slave-riddled globalization, "derivatives," and "subprime mortgages" were whipped up like modern witches' brews. That is the way with classical literature and great poetry. It gets to the deepest predicates of human personality and so finds enduring and universal application. It also divines innate human flaws and fatal moral fault lines.

The Occupy Wall Street protesters and the Hebrew prophets discerned a penchant in human society for power and wealth to move to the top, propelled by violent greed. Gerhard E. Lenski, in his study of social stratification, shows the historic persistence of one-percent greedalism. In nineteenth-century China, the figure for the monopolists at the top of the economic pyramid was 1.3 percent, in nineteenth-century Russia, 1.25 percent. In the last days of the Roman Republic, one percent had the strangling grip on wealth. The same pattern prevailed in ancient China, India, Turkey, Japan, Persia, and in Hammurabi's Babylon.[8] It seems inscribed into us like a recessive moral gene.

What is contained in the first twenty-four chapters of Exodus has been called the first ideologically based sociopolitical revolution in the history of the world.[9] George E. Mendenhall says, "discontent movements are a constant as shown by the history of revolt, war, and rebellion. But rare indeed are those movements in history that result in such creative breaks with the past that they survive for centuries and expand over large population areas to create some sort of social unity or unified tradition that did not exist before. The first such movement to survive was the biblical one."[10] This does not mean it is the best the world has to offer nor can it pretend to having all the answers to unfolding life, but it is a signal phenomenon that deserves attention in a world suffering vision-famine. It did, however, have a revolutionary substance in its genetic makeup. Lenski, who was not filing a brief for any religion, comments that "the religions of the East, especially Hinduism and Confucianism, were compatible with extremes of exploitation in a way that Judaism and Christianity were not."[11] As mentioned earlier, Marx saw this and the Marxian principle "that rewards should be distributed 'to each according to his needs,' is almost a direct quotation from the Acts of the Apostles (4:35) in which the practice of the early Christian community in Jerusalem is described."[12]

But Where Was God in All of This?

All this occurred in a world not yet ready for atheism. Gods were always fashioned to handle the tough jobs and to lend credibility to risky undertakings and adventures. Certainly a well-credentialed and innovative god was needed by the Israelites to help with what they audaciously set out to do. What they set out to do was to constitute an egalitarian social system in the midst of stratified, hierarchical societies, and to make that system survive against all odds in the Canaanite highlands for at least two centuries . . . with resonance into our very day. Such an agenda called for a special god indeed and Yahweh was fitted out for the task. All the other gods had to be ousted—and the prophets railed against them—because all of them were bred of feudal models.

Yahweh was fashioned as "the symbol of a single-minded pursuit of an egalitarian tribal social system, a symbol carved out of a common pool of ancient Near Eastern belief in individuated high gods," but the people were not to serve this god so much as this god was to serve the people. Yahweh was fashioned and polished to suit Israel's revolutionary purposes.[13] The title Yahweh, coming from an etymological root that means one who can make it happen, gave numinous authorization to the grand experiment. As Gottwald says, "all of the symbols of Yahweh in his various guise refer with positive reinforcement to socioeconomic *desiderata* in the community" and to give assurance that the anti-feudal, anti-hierarchical, egalitarian system they were pioneering would survive.

Gods were in the air the Hebrews breathed but the philosophy that developed was anterior to the god-talk and god imagery. The motley pantheon and the evolving god-talk need not distract us from the revolution of social theory that unfolded. Gottwald recognizes that the form of political consciousness that emerged from this creative people is "separable from beliefs in gods as personal beings or as invisible forces."[14] In fact, as Morton Smith notes, in the world of early Israel, there was "no general term for religion." In its world, Judaism "was a philosophy," a "cult of wisdom." *Philosophy* is the best term to describe the literary and political eruption that was Israel.[15] This is Judaism's self-portrait in Deuteronomy: "You will display your wisdom and understanding to other peoples. When they hear about these statutes, they will say, 'What a wise and understanding people this great nation is!'" (Deut. 4:6). These people were onto something and they were confident the world would come to appreciate it. Their confidence was not entirely in vain. As Morton Smith says, this little movement became "the seedbed of the subsequent religious history of the Western world."[16] And that religious history was a constant interactive influence on political and economic history.

The Arrogance of Genius

The prophets of Israel saw no reason to be humble about their ideas. Isaiah told the people of Israel that when their social experiment became known, the other nations of the world, all of them, "shall march toward your light and their kings to your sunrise" (Isa. 60:3). It must have amused the haughty courts of surrounding powers to hear that this ragtag bunch of rebels thought it has a sunrise toward which they and all of history should march! Jeremiah matched Isaiah's assurance: He felt his work was nothing less that establishing a new world order. Accordingly he claimed "authority over nations and over kingdoms, to pull down and to uproot, to destroy and to demolish, to build and to plant" (Jer. 1:10). Jesus, too, was immodest to the point of bombast when he instructed his followers to turn all the nations of the world into his students, "make all nations my disciples" because "full authority in heaven and on earth has been committed to me" (Matt. 28:18).

The grandness of these claims marks the grandness of the project begun at Sinai. Their business was to challenge systems that left the underclass groaning under the overclass. To address this you had to talk "kings" and "nations." A thousand points of individual do-gooder lights would not cut it. The change needed was systemic, not patchwork. As these poets put it, "Every valley shall be filled in, and every mountain and hill leveled; the corners shall be straightened, and the rugged ways made smooth" (Luke 3:5). It was not a matter of minor repairs; the goal was "new heavens and a new earth" (Isa. 65:17).

Now people claiming authority over nations and kingdoms and poetizing about leveling mountains and filling valleys could be delusional. The only thing that could save them from looking silly and manic would be if their poetic re-envisioning of life attained to classical excellence. Classics do have authority over heaven and earth because of the in-depth penetration they make into the mysteries of truth and beauty. Now much of the Bible is gibberish and neither the Hebrew nor the Christian scriptures were well pruned when they were put together into a definitive canon. But like a Gulf Stream that persists undeterred by storms, the Exodus Sinai revolution of consciousness kept reasserting itself through the pages of this literature and deserves a place among other literary classics of human insight and sensibility.[17]

What Makes a Classic a Classic

The term *classic* has been vulgarized in usage to mean such things as a certain type of Coca-Cola or a well-pitched baseball game. Against this usage scholars have labored to preserve the category to describe moments when the human mind peaks in its grasp of the true, the good, and the beautiful. There is no classical, canonical agreement of what makes a classic a classic, but there do seem to be certain qualities without which the term *classic* would seem a compliment misapplied. I would offer five of these: *excellence, universalizability, shock, hope*, and *fecundity*.

Excellence. David Tracy says, "certain expressions of the human spirit so disclose a compelling truth about our lives that we cannot deny them some kind of normative status. Thus do we name these expressions and these alone, 'classics.'"[18] The opposite of the classic is the period piece, the fad, the momentary, the provincial, or things with glitzy and tawdry celebrity. The excellence of the classic is such that it seems to enjoy an inexhaustibility of meaning. It admits of deepening connoisseurship and some of its signals are of such high decibel that only with scholarly guidance can they be heard.

Universalizability. Frank Kermode speaks of "perpetual contemporaneity" as a mark of the classic. When a classic speaks, as Virgil did, we know in it "the voice of a metropolitan whole of which we are but provincial parts."[19] Classics melt borders geographically and temporally. They are as at home in today as they were in yesterday—and maybe even more so as new developments make their insights even more relevant and more obviously true.

Shock. Superimposed on our individual lenses are the lenses of the culture in which we live. Those lenses might enhance our vision but they can also narrow it. The need for cognitive security, unthreatened by too much newness, is such that the tendency to constrict is dominant. The cultural lenses can tyrannize our imagination and straiten our focus. Racist, sexist, classist lenses are fitted onto our toddler eyes.

Enter the classic. The classic jostles our lenses and unleashes what Michel Foucault calls an "insurrection of subjugated knowledges."[20] Once again, what Herbert Marcuse says of art applies: "Whether ritualized or not, art contains the rationality of negation. In its advanced positions, it is the Great Refusal—the protest against that which is."[21] In a classic, the *might be* triumphs over the grip of the stale status quo. Classics are subversive of the petty and sectarian orthodoxies and ideologies that form like crusts, keeping out both light and clean air.

Hope. Hope follows like a corollary to all of the above. The experience of an excellence that has universal appeal and that shocks us toward previously unsuspected horizons is hope-engendering. The opposite of hope is paralysis and a classic is beauty and truth in motion; it catches us in its swirl. It enlarges our sense of possibility and invites participation.

Fecundity. Classics are fruitful in two ways: they spawn other classics, and in the hands of new masters more is found in them than was even suspected by their original authors. Classics are perennials that rise to new life with each new vernal opportunity. Millennia later their insights may be vindicated as they could not be at the time of their creation. In the presence of a classic, standards rise and thus critical thought is encouraged. No wonder dictators ban and censor them; they are antidotal to any slavery of the mind. They break shackles and allow the lame to walk.

It is my contention that the Exodus/Sinai epic, a poetic epic unfolding through the Hebrew and the Christian scriptures, achieves *classical* power. Put aside a literal, nonmetaphoric reading of the ragged and never fully successful move from polytheism to monolatry, to a troubled monotheism with polytheistic undertones and triune gods. Put all that aside. These are metaphors mistaken as supernal people. They only serve when they are seen as metaphors for a creative people's struggle for newness and liberation. Only in that way can the Exodus/Sinai classic take its place among the world's other classics.

Pragmatic Utopianism

One of life's greatest frustrations is telling a really funny joke to humorless persons; they just don't get it. Moving from a prose reading to a poetic reading of the biblical literature involves comparable pain. The task grows harder if the poetry is a summons to be free, to shake the shackles of paltry expectations, but let's have at it. Walter Brueggemann is a master guide and I will ride upon his shoulders. Says Brueggemann, the Bible is poetry and "the intention of the poetry is to create an edginess that propels listeners out beyond their comfort zone." The purpose of the poetry is "to mobilize the displaced to new possibility, to summon them out beyond the assumptions" that tyrannize their minds and their political institutions. Even Yahweh speaks 'in poetic utterance."[22] The Hebrews were the poets who broke the shackles of "normalcy."

What's more, this ancient poetry is screamingly relevant today. "This narrative reads like it had been written yesterday." The insights are "acutely contemporary"; these writings have an "urgent contemporaneity" speaking pointedly to our bungled and proliferating international crises.[23] Great poetry is never the captive of any moment. The Exodus/Sinai epic "moves out beyond Israel" and reveals "the narrative quality of the entire human historical process."[24]

Modern sophisticates can deride the misplaced simplicities of ancient faith while mimicking them. "American exceptionalism" houses an ancient deviant creed reborn "in which liberals and conservatives together take for granted our privileged status in the world as God's most recently chosen people."[25]

The figures of Pharaoh and Solomon are types that keep on recurring, to be coped with in every age. It's hard for America, the land of the free and the home of the brave, to think of itself as imprisoned in Pharaoh's Egypt and needing to escape. We are seduced by what Brueggemann calls "the triad of death," *spin, power*, and *wealth*. That's the perennial pharaonic formula for enthroning greedy accumulation at the pinnacle of the pyramid where the one percent wallows in purloined privileges.

As Brueggemann says, the ancient Pharaoh "is a metaphor in the Hebrew Bible as the paradigmatic enemy of the common good, an agent of immense power who could not get beyond his acquisitive interests to ponder the common good."[26] The Pharaoh is the 1 percent who reappears in every age as monarch, king, or corporation, siphoning power and wealth to the top, leaving 99 percent in a subordinated supportive role. You see this model's enduring contemporaneity when Joesph Stiglitz reports that in the United States the top 1 percent of income earners took home 93 percent of the growth in incomes in 2010. The base of the pyramid, the 99 percent, saw their income shrink. You see this same pharaonic strategem when the United Nations Development Programme reports in 1992 that 82.7 percent of world income goes to the richest 20 percent leaving 17.3 percent of world income for the rest of humanity. The results are not kind. In the United States, more than a fifth of our children live in poverty—the second worst of all the advanced economies. That even puts us behind countries like Bulgaria, Latvia, and Greece.

Under the confusing term of *neoliberalism* the reverse Robin Hood effect is ritualized. According to Margaret Thatcher business must be "given vent"; giving vent to the oligarchs is pure neoliberal dogma. In pre-Thatcher Britain, about one person in ten was below the poverty line; when she finished giving vent, one person in four and one child in three was officially poor.[27]

The system is seriously irrational as well as barbaric. In the United States, says Stiglitz, "The growth in the decade before the crisis was unsustainable—it was reliant on the bottom 80 percent consuming about 110 percent of their income."[28] Pharaonic math was bad then and it is bad now. It tries to suck water out of the very base it is desiccating. A bit nutty, really, but still in vogue.[29] It did it in 1928 when the top 1 percent received 25 percent of the income and then came 1928; it had done it again by 2007 when the same disproportion obtained—and then came the enduring recession of 2008.

The Democracy Illusion

Wealth does not shift naturally from bottom to top as cream rises in a pitcher. The fix is in, and skilled busy hands are at work on it. Elections do not a democracy make and real power is wise enough to realize that. In power terms, "we the people," that is, we the people with our hands on the controls, is a very small "we." In allegedly democratic America it is class not *demos* who rule. Michael Zweig writes that in terms of real power "the entire U.S. ruling class could fit into the seats of the old Yankee Stadium (capacity 54,000)."[30] These are corporate directors who sit on multiple boards, the political elites in the three branches of national government, and those cultural and educational leaders who contribute to the furtherance of corporate interests. We do not call them nobles or lords, much less the court of Pharaoh, but greedy dominance by any other name doth smell as foul.

Poetry is not the foe of realism. It does not exclude the practicality of experience-bred cynicism. But it just doesn't stop there. It struggles to see more deeply into the real and into what really might be. Enter the Sinai alternative to which I now turn.

CHAPTER 12

WHEN HISTORY TURNED A CORNER

In political and economic ethics, it is the simplest truths that are most often neglected. In his *Nichomachean Ethics* Aristotle said it is justice, and only justice, that holds the city together.[1] If injustice reigns, the fibers that bind are unraveled and unstrung. Thomas Aquinas, commenting on Aristotle, summed up with comparable simplicity what justice is: "Justice consists in sharing."[2] Every surviving polity in history operated out of a vision of justice. They either established certain patterns of sharing or they crumbled.

Ancient societies spun mythic tales about their origins. These tales (always wrapped in god-talk signaling their seriousness), varied in quality and longevity. The Jewish philosopher Michael Walzer credits the Exodus/Sinai epic with an almost unmatchable success. It is, he said, the taproot of all revolutions in the modern world. It established a symbolic pattern that worked into the social imagination of diverse literate cultures.

> The pharaonic oppression, deliverance, Sinai, and Canaan are still with us, powerful memories shaping our perceptions of the political world. The "door of hope" is still open; things

> are not what they might be. . . . This is a central theme in Western thought, always present though elaborated in many different ways. We still believe, or many of us do, what the Exodus first taught, or what it has commonly been taken to teach, about the meaning and possibility of politics and about its proper form.[3]

As Walzer says, wherever you live, it is probably Egypt, but the myth says there is a better place, a promised land and the way to get there is through the struggles of a "wilderness" that cannot be traversed without "joining together and marching" through rough desert terrain.

Hannah Arendt asserts that there was a revolutionary substance even in the Christian belief in an afterlife. "The Christian 'glad tiding' of the immortality of individual human life had reversed the ancient relationship between [human beings] and the world and promoted the most mortal thing, human life, to the position of immortality, which up to then the cosmos had held."[4] Prior to that, when death seemed ever crouched under the lintel, ready to strike, the precarious value of individual human life was easily subsumed into the more stable collectivity. Individual citizens were like waves. They rose, crested impressively perhaps, but then sank without leaving a trace. The ocean remained. Romans died: *Roma dea* did not. The hypothesis of immortality challenged that; it was a symbolic protest against the divine claims of the state. The literal interpretation of "afterlife" misses that.

The Passover memory of the myth of Exodus, says Walter Brueggemann, became—and not only for Jews—"a paradigmatic narrative through which all social reality is described and re-experienced." It is a narrative that got down to brass tacks, not eschewing details, and is credited with becoming "the first move toward a social safety net in the history of the world."[5] This is what epics do—or can do—and in this case the epic did it—seemingly with unparalleled force in Western culture. Claiming uniqueness is not the point. Power is the point and the biblical epic was charged with it. It did not get born and die without issue. Philosopher Eric Voegelin sees that just as Israel was a political threat to neighboring feudal regimes, so, too, Christianity evoked persecution from monarchs. "The Christians were persecuted for a good reason; there was a revolutionary substance in Christianity that made it incompatible" with the surrounding cultures. "What made Christianity so dangerous was its uncompromising, radical de-divinization of the world."[6] The currently given was not destiny, and that was the prime meaning of the Exodus/Sinai epic. It has not yet appeared what we can be.

The Pharaonic Alternative

Pharaoh was the symbol of the dominant alternative narrative, a narrative that is still very much in play in the inchoate struggles for true democracy among modern nations. In the government of corporations and alleged democracies, Pharaoh rules. The pharaonic formula: *accumulation by the few, with order maintained by force and fear, and the stifling of that most revolutionary sentiment, hope.* But the poetry of Exodus and the principles developed at Sinai sang a new and antidotal song of liberation and sowed the seeds of democratic theory. Recall that Engels saw the biblical experiment in political economy as presaging the rise of socialism, harboring as it did the "seditious" power to undermine imperialism.[7]

Idealism with an Eye to the Bottom Line

The Hebrews were not whifty idealists. Their idealism had its roots in the world of flesh and blood and dirt where values ultimately live. Theirs was a *do good to do well* plan, a moral mandate with a payload. You can see this in a single text in Isaiah, 32:17, a foundational text deserving two Nobel prizes, one in economics and one in peace. It states the case directly: *unless you plant Sedaqah you will not have Shalom, unless you plant the form of justice that institutionalizes sharing to eliminate poverty you will not have security and peace.* The text is echoed in Matthew's gospel: if you focus on "justice . . . the rest will come to you as well" (Matt. 6:33). That is all happy talk unless you get down to details, and the Hebrews did:

Rule one: *poverty is social cancer and it must go.* "There shall be no poor among you" (Deut. 15:4). The chosen biblical metaphor for a society (applicable now to an interconnected planet), is the *household*. Bible scholar Douglas Meeks says: "Will everyone in the household get what it takes to live? This is the first and last question of economics" from the biblical perspective.[8]

Again, justice consists in sharing.

Never underestimate the incisive power of a metaphor. A cartoonist captured the simple wisdom of the household metaphor. The cartoon pictured a family of five seated around the kitchen table with bills and a checkbook before them. The father says: "I've called you all together to let you know that because of inflation, I'm going to have to let two of you go." The message is commonsensical as well as comical because we don't dump people in a household. We rearrange patterns of sharing so as not to sacrifice some to others. The society that does not share is practicing human sacrifice.

Monique "Nikki" White was a "bright, feisty, dazzling young woman" who, fresh out of college, contracted systemic lupus erythermatosus, a serious condition but one that can be managed by modern medicine. Because she had too much money to qualify for health care under welfare but had too little to pay for the drugs and doctors she needed to stay alive, she died at age thirty-two. Had she lived in any other well-off country, like Japan, Germany, Britain, France, Italy, Spain, Canada, Sweden, and so on, she could have lived. Nikki White's misfortune was to live in the world's richest country, the United States of America. Because of that she died.[9] When you don't share well, you practice human sacrifice.

Nikki White's case illustrates another point of the biblical poets: injustice is stupid. At the end of her life when she was destitute and eligible for Medicaid, she had had more than twenty-five operations and intensive care.[10] It was too late. She died. And this futile last minute care cost more than treating her and keeping her alive would have cost. The prophets repeatedly addressed this stupidity of ours: "Have you eyes and cannot see, ears and cannot hear?"

Household versus Jungle

At the antipodes of "household" is the "ideology of beneficent cupidity," as Richard Hofstadter called it, and that ideology is the central dogma of neoliberalism.[11] Neoliberalism, for all its claims to realism, is a blind faith that believes, in the teeth of inveterate contrary evidence, that greed will erect a cornucopia from which good will trickle down to one and all. There is no manna for the poor, however, in the neoliberal desert and "sharing" is called *redistribution*, the dirtiest word for neoliberal fundamentalists.

The Hebrews did not share this strategic neoliberal naiveté: they knew that systemic problems need systemic cures—and massive poverty is systemic, not the personal achievement of masses hell-bent on achieving their own destitution. The social architects at Sinai put in place that nemesis of right wing thinking, *redistribution*. They knew what Jefferson would later state—that where there are multitudes of dispossessed poor "it is clear that the laws of property have been so far extended as to violate natural right."[12]

What drove and distinguished this Hebraic movement was hope. Other slaves suffered and bent their heads to the ground; they saw no exit and no horizon. As Gerhard Lenski points out, peasant revolts in history are remarkably rare since the deck was so mightily stacked against them.[13] Despair is the *sine qua non* base of tyranny and tyranny knows how to stir it. Tyranny requires TINA, the belief that "There Is No Alternative." Exodus was TAAA; *There Are Always Alternatives*. There is a promised land, but you will wander in the desert forever if you don't get directions; this poetry got down to brass tacks and directions.

Regulation and Taxation, Hebrew Style

"Regulations" is another word hated today by the keepers of the *greedocracy*. It takes regulation to move society from a pharaonic oligarchy to a humane prosperity. Since some people are luckier and some are pluckier, lopsided inequality happens with the force of gravity. So the Hebrews took to social planning. Every seventh year was designated the "sabbatical year." Debts—even honest and fair debts—should be canceled and all slaves should be released (Deut. 15:12–18). Since that would not be enough, every fiftieth year would be the "jubilee year." If people had lost their land though bankruptcy, it was to be restored to them. The plan is that "each man shall dwell under his own vine, under his own fig-tree undisturbed" (Mic. 4:4). "The poverty of the poor is their ruin," says Proverbs 10:15, but it ruins the rest of us, too.

Aside from the mandated sharing of jubilee and sabbatical, farmers are told never to reap all of their harvest, neither should they strip their vineyards or glean all the fallen grapes. "You shall leave them for the poor and the immigrant" (Lev. 19:10). Hospitality is to be extended to runaway slaves (Deut. 23:15–16). No collateral is to be required on loans made to poor people (Deut. 24:10–13).

And there is more: every third year a tenth of all the year's produce was to be laid up in the towns so that the poor could "come and eat their fill" (Deut. 14:29). Note "their fill": nothing stinting about the generosity of justice. One of the most morally loaded terms in the human lexicon is the word *own*. At Sinai, this pregnant word *own* was civilized and tempered by social need. There is, as Pope John Paul II put it, a "social mortgage" on ownership. Owing is morally conjoined to owning. Abraham Heschel puts it this way, that in the biblical tradition "one senses owingness rather than ownership." To be truly human requires a "consciousness of indebtedness."[14] As Warren Buffett says, he could not have built his business in the Gobi desert. We are born owing, and our debts keep mounting. Gratitude is essential to a social conscience. The right to private property is natural, every one under their own vine and fig tree, but that right is relative, not absolute. The right to "private property" is not an island. It exists in creative tension with social need. The biblical morality epic saw sociality as essential to personhood standing on a par with our need for privacy and individuality. We are neighborly animals who cannot get conceived or develop or thrive as isolates.

In the Exodus/Sinai epic, redistribution is not selfless generosity. It's a *do it, or suffer the consequences* deal. Isaiah heaps scorn on greedy accumulators who half-wittedly pretend that they "dwell alone in the land," piling up wealth with no thought of the common good. The result of such untrammeled accumulation is "ruin" (Isa. 5:89). Try it and "down go nobility and common people" alike (Isa. 5:14). Greed, like all tyrannies, implodes. (Again, think 1929 and 2008 . . . again, the striking contemporaneity of these insights.)

"Wonder Bread"

The poetic nature of the Exodus/Sinai narrative shines clearly in the story of the "manna" bread that wondrously appeared in the desert to feed the escaping slaves. Walter Brueggemann explains its symbolism. "Manna" means "What is it?" The answer is: it was a lesson in economics. It gave economic standing to the word *enough* and it mocked hoarding. Anxiety produces hoarding and Moses condemned it. Of the bread he said, "Let no one leave any of it over until morning" (Exod. 16:19). The people did not heed this. They filled their pockets and baskets with this bread lest there be none tomorrow. "They did not listen to Moses; some left part of it until morning, and it bred worms and became foul. Moses was angry with them. Morning by morning they gathered it, as much as each needed; but when the sun grew hot, it melted" (Exod. 16:20–21). The lesson, poetically delivered, is that excesses of wealth hoarded and not adequately shared for the common good turn foul and wormy and suffer meltdown.[15] The manna story is of a piece with the sabbatical year and the jubilee. It's another way of getting at the greed thing. Miss the poetry and you miss the message.

Recidivism

The Exodus/Sinai epic does not see the move from predatory economy to shared prosperity as easy. In poetic form it shows the allure of chains. Personal good tends to trump the common good because we forget that the common good is the setting of all private good. The poets of Israel honed in on this tangentially fatal flaw. First of all, it was hard to get the people to move out of pharaonic bondage in Egypt and once out they wanted to go back. Brueggemann notes that the travel out of Egypt into the alternative narrative "immediately produces an attack of nostalgia for the imagined good old days of Pharaoh." Israel found the "new narrative too demanding."[16] People are easily seduced into voting for their oppressors in times ancient and modern. Reflective of this, Solomon married Pharaoh's daughter and Egypt returned to Israel. Forced labor, class differentiation, and militarism followed, replacing the prophetic dream of poverty banished and swords turned into plowshares.[17]

The prophetic poets could not be silent in the face of all this. Nathan took on Solomon and mocked his pharaonic mimicry (2 Sam. 12:1–5). Elijah, called a "troubler" and "enemy," clashed with the pharaonic Ahab (1 Kings 18:17; 21:20); Amos spoke blunt truth to the pharaonic Amaziah (Amos 7:10–17). These prophets, says Brueggemann, should not be called "great liberals. They were, rather, poets outside the box" who were rooted in Sinai, and they screamed maledictions at the reemergence of a predatory economy.[18] They would have none of that "lethal silence" that legitimates tyranny. Small wonder that human history is splattered with prophets' blood. Like fish swimming in swillish waters, we will bite that hand that would move us to fresh streams of possibility.

But What of the Rest of Nature?

Early ecological sensibilities appear, in spite of the Bible's strong anthropocentrism. In the swirl of history, ideals never appear full blown. They push out through the clay and peek out like tiny shoots, unexpected, plaintive protests against the established patterns. Thus slavery was not entirely eliminated but it was limited to seven years by the sabbatical rules. Similarly the Sinai vision was not wholly unaware of the rest of nature as its kith and kin. Some ecological sensitivities were breaking through. Every seventh year the land is to be left in untilled peace: "The land shall keep a Sabbath of sacred rest." Much of the land will still be producing but what is produced should be shared with strangers and kin, but also with animals, domestic and wild (Lev. 25:5–7). Joy is our destiny and all of nature should share in it. "The mountains and the hills before you shall burst into song, and all the trees of the fields shall clap their hands; instead of the thorn shall come up the cypress, instead of the brier shall come up the myrtle" (Isa. 55:12–13).

The Power Curve

No philosophy of life can fail to address power.[19] Power has a wide range from violent to nonviolent and the Bible runs the gamut. In so doing it illustrates again the rough birthing of ideals. Remember that god-talk encapsulates our deepest convictions. In the Hebrew's early history, their god was often a brute. In the Song of Moses he is one tough deity. "The Lord is a warrior . . . majestic in strength" who lets loose "fury" and unleashes the "blast" of divine "anger" (Exod. 15:3–8). Bloody crusaders and slavers ran to the Bible to find support for their truculence and they found it aplenty.

But something happened in the saga of Israel. Abraham Heschel could say that the Israelites "were the first [people] in history to regard a nation's reliance upon force as evil."[20]

How then did they get from a god who went to war with the fury of a volcano to filing a brief against violent power? Practicality was their first step. These were poets who could do cost/benefit analyses. They early on reached the conclusion that violence is counterproductive—it bites back at you. "Dismayed are those" who rely on it (Hab. 1:11). In a hostile world the people wanted to be saved but they reached the conclusion that "neither by force of arms nor by brute strength" would that happen (Zech. 4:6). "Not by might shall a man prevail" (1 Sam. 2:9). They predicted that military power will be discredited. "The nations shall see and be ashamed of all their might" (Mic. 7:16). "The song of the military (ruthless)" will be silenced and fortified cities will become a ruin (Isa. 25:5, 2). And then that most stunning prediction of a world without war emerging from a world that was full of war: "They shall beat their swords into mattocks and their spears into pruning-knives; nation shall not lift sword against nation nor ever again be trained for war" (Isa. 2:4). Presciently, these very practical poets began to see that violent power is the most delusional and least successful mode of power. It can at times be necessary in policing situations, but it cannot dominate your power repertoire. Try it and you will fall on your sword.[21]

Yahweh as Convert

Since gods mirror their creators, Yahweh had a change of heart. No longer the warrior, his mind and his behavior changed. Horses and chariots were the state-of-the-art weapons, and now Yahweh hated them. "Horses and chariots are a threat to the social experiment which is Israel . . . Yahweh is the sworn enemy of such modes of power."[22] He got preachy about it: "you cannot build Zion in bloodshed" (Mic. 3:10). "I will break bow and sword and weapons of war and sweep them off the earth, so that all living creatures may lie down without fear" (Hos. 2:18). Notice that the message was "for all living creatures," not just for Israel. These people thought big. Isaiah admitted that this was "a new thing." To make his case, he reminded them of what happened to Pharaoh's horses and chariots. They were drawn to their destruction, "a whole army, men of valor; there they lay never to rise again; they were crushed, snuffed out like a wick." Forget those old modes of power. "Cease to dwell on days gone by and to brood over past history. Here and now I will do a new thing; this moment it will break from the bud. Can you not perceive it?" (Isa. 43:16–20). The image of the bud suggests the delicate birthing of this new vision, the slow birthing of a new moral and political reality. Another insight more relevant today than when it was first written.

But were Isaiah and the other poets having pipe dreams? Face it: that bud of theirs was slow to blossom. Their world was awash in bloody violence. So is ours. Nevertheless—and amazingly—they saw the possibility of civilizing power before such intelligent restraint was practicable. But suddenly, in our day, that vision is displaying the contemporaneity of a classic insight. The facts on the ground are now more ready; the ideal is becoming a practical necessity.

Francis Fukuyama's "end of history" was a rhetorical overstretch, but Andrew Bacevich, cited earlier, a man schooled in war at West Point and in Vietnam, sees what might be the end of "military history" as we have known it. In the twentieth century, the nations of the world went broke perfecting and amassing weapons of coercion. Their frenzy was based on the "common belief in the plausibility of victory." War was still "a viable instrument of statecraft," and even more so given the technical "accouterments of modernity." But, alas, those very accouterments undercut the utility of salvific slaughter. War demanded too much and gave too little. "Pain vastly exceeded gain." The war of 1914–1918 was emblematic of it; "even the winners ended up losers." By 1945 most nations lost faith in "war's problem-solving capacity." Among nations "classified as liberal democracies, only two resisted this trend": the United States and Israel. They placed their bets on "unambiguous military superiority." The 1967 war seemed to prove it for Israel and the 1991 "Desert Storm" seemed to vindicate American faith in arms over diplomacy.

But Bacevich says both victories were illusory and the glow short-lived. Israel became shackled "to a rapidly growing and resentful Palestinian population that it could neither pacify nor assimilate." And the United States' effort to pacify and control the Middle East failed. No one could doubt American and Israeli military dominance, but Bacevich asked the disarming question: "So what?" By 2007, American military leaders had shelved their expectations of winning (in the Rabin or Schwarzkopf mode) and sought instead not to lose. "Avoidance of outright defeat emerged as the new gold standard of success."[23] And both countries remain on "orange alert," two Goliaths fearing little Davids. The Goliaths have no answer to the Davids' guerilla tactics with drones now added to the guerillas' repertoire.

Gorbachev had spoken shrewdly, toward the end of the Soviet Union, when he said that war had moved from the battlefield to the market place. Better yet the Chinese official who said with a wry smile: "You Americans invade oil rich countries. We simply buy the oil. It's cheaper and no one gets hurt." He could have added, "but if you insist on the ways of war, we will lend you the money to do that at handsome interest and we will use that interest to buy oil, invest in poor countries with mineral resources, and practice the old 'dollar diplomacy' you Americans once perfected and then abandoned in favor of kill-power." And old Isaiah would nod derisively at all that naive reliance on aggressive violence, and say "I told you so already! Have you eyes and cannot see? Have you ears and cannot hear?"

Isaiah *redivivus* may have referred the United States and Israel to the king of Israel who dealt with the hostile Aramaeans. The prophet Elisha brought some of the Aramaeans to the king and the king asked the prophet if he should slay them. The prophet had a different approach to these enemies. "Give them food and water and let them eat and drink, and then go back to their master." So the king "prepared a great feast for them and they ate and drank and then went back to their master. And Aramaean raids on Israel ceased" (2 Kings 6:20–23). The king had it in his power to kill them; the poetic prophet taught him that there was power also in knowing the enemies' needs and addressing them with the arts of diplomacy. "And Aramaean raids on Israel ceased." After the 9/11 attacks, a little girl was quoted in the newspapers as asking: "Why do they hate us so much they will die to hurt us?" Had she been answered thoughtfully the results may have been more effective than military flailings and "shock and awe." There was no Elisha there to tell the American king not to slay them but to feed them with a determined effort to know their grievances real and imagined; and so the American king turned to slaying and the Aramaeans continue to attack.

The Hope Dividend

One would not think that poor medieval farmers, bowed over the furrow and the plow, would have turned to poetry for relief and for hope, but that is what they did. Herbert Marcuse, a socialist philosopher, praised the role of the majestic medieval cathedrals, like Chartres. People labored on those for generations carrying stones after long days in the field. That's how these mighty classics rose at the edges of humble little towns. These edifices were poems in stone and glass and metal. They did what poetry can do. Again, as Marcuse said, "Art contains the rationality of negation. . . . It is the Great Refusal—the protest against that which is."[24] Art is an Exodus experience. The farmer sweating in the field could look up at these temples of beauty and see that there is more to life than labor and pain. Marcuse puts it even more enigmatically when he says, "That which is cannot be true."[25] Our *can be* gets strangled by our *is*. Poetic vision is medicinal to this catatonia.

When the biblical poets spoke of "the reign of God" they were building a cathedral at the edge of town. "Reign of God" meant a whole new way of living. The "reign of God" symbol signaled a crashing against an inadequate present and a pull toward a fantastically different yet plausible future. They were calling for drastically new "habits of the heart" and mind, and they used stark images to jar minds. Going after their skewed and paltry affections, Jeremiah urged his people to "remove the foreskin of [their] hearts" and to wash those circumcised hearts from small think (Jer. 4:4, 14). To pull people out of imprisoning ruts, all customary ways of thinking had to be jettisoned. Highways must be built through the rough deserts of our minds. Mountains must be made into valleys and valleys into mountains (Isa. 40:3–5; Luke 3:4–6). The opening cry of the earliest gospel is *metanoiete* (Mark 1:14). This Greek word means, literally, a change of mind, but in the Semitic cast of this literature, it takes on stronger emotive content. It calls for a shift in feeling, a new relationship to the truth, and it demands a painful divorce from previous attitudes and behavior.[26]

The practical biblical poets recognize, sometimes impatiently, that this will not be easy. "Have you no inkling yet? . . . Are your minds closed?" (Mark 8:17–18). Security, however precarious, is a hazard; it blinds us to the possibility of a society reformed and reimagined. "It is easier for a camel to pass through the eye of a needle than for a rich man to enter the kingdom of God," with "kingdom of God" symbolizing this new liberated mentality (Mark 10:25). The axe must be laid to the root of old mental habits (Luke 3:9). The difficulty of moving to a higher, more humane level of consciousness and social arrangements is even said to be like going back into the womb and being born all over again (John 3:4). Clearly this literature does not underestimate its own radicality.

The Four Synoptic Gospels

In spite of dogmatic differences between the Hebrew and Christian scriptures, there is an enduring moral-political Exodus *leitmotif* in these traditions. Significantly all four gospels begin with Isaiah, chapter 40, and its promise that a road can be cleared through the wilderness of our contrivances and the mountains and valleys can be transformed. "Rugged places shall be made smooth . . . and all humankind shall see it" (Isa. 40:2–3). Those who accept this dare, who act out on this vision, "will win new strength, they will grow wings like eagles; they will run and not be weary, they will march on and never grow faint" (v. 31). This chapter, which is so eloquent on the hopes born in Israel, presents the vision in god-speak because god-speak always lends authority. They were saying this epic narrative of human possibility "is the voice of your God." Therefore, "listen up!"

Historically people did listen and history turned little corners. There is a lot in our times that should open our ears to this symphony of biblical good-sense poetry. The apparent naiveté of the biblical poets is seeming more like hard-nosed realism. Momentous changes are well on. Woman-spirit is rising like it never did in human history; it is acting like a solvent on macho poisons that infected all the halls of social power. For the first time in history human problems are global and cannot be solved in the anarchic arrangement of supposedly sovereign independent states initiated at Westphalia in another time for another purpose. According to Norman K. Gottwald, early Israel got the power to challenge Egyptian imperialism and city-state feudalism by uniting tribal groups. Previously they were stymied by "the dominant system, a system which astutely employed its tight organization at the top to separate and to splinter restive groups at the bottom and on the fringes." The solution was to transcend the previous fragmentation and link up "exploited peoples across the boundaries of the old city-state division."[27] Nations are modern tribes and they suffer from fragmentation. These artifacts can yield, and must, to permit a new political/economic globalization of cooperative power.

Supposedly sovereign states cannot stop the melting of glaciers that could raise sea levels 3 feet by the year 2100. Kill-power is frustrated by its own Frankensteinian progress that has made "military victory" a chimaera. Nonviolent power is proving more effective. Gene Sharp lists 198 successes of nonviolent power that historians have neglected, preferring to report on the flash of war. Britain's Indian colony of three hundred million people was liberated nonviolently and it cost about eight thousand lives. France's Algerian colony of about ten million people was liberated violently but it cost almost one million lives.[28] Do the math.

"Labor arbitrage," the euphemism for the enslavement of surplus workers in weaker nations, is meeting opposition and exposure and does not show long-term viability. The Internet, possibly the greatest leap forward since the invention of writing five thousand years ago, brings disinfecting sunlight to corners that despots in corporations and government want to keep dark. The stage is urgently set for a moral-political-economic Exodus and a Sinai set of new rules for internationalizing to help nations grow out of their adolescent and obsolete illusion of independence. They might find that cultural differences could still flourish in a matrix of human unity. And it is starting to happen. As Jonathan Schell writes: "National sovereignty is now in the process of giving way to new forces in the very Europe in which the concept was born."[29] From Kenya comes a supporting voice: "I believe that the world has moved closer to oneness and more people see each other as one with the other. . . . It is possible to have new thoughts and new common values for humans and all other forms of life."[30]

Hope is not dead, even in our battered corner of the universe. Changes we have made that beat the odds should heal our numbing ennui. Take heart from David Korten's observation: "Consider the ridicule that would have been heaped on the visionary who dared even in 1988 to predict that by 1991 the Soviet Union would peacefully dissolve itself, Germany would be reunited, the Berlin Wall would be gone and the leadership of the former 'evil empire' would be inviting the United States to help dismantle is nuclear arsenal."[31] Who could have predicted the Good Friday Accord in Ireland, the election of Nelson Mandela as President of South Africa, and Barack Obama elected and reelected president? Simple ideas beckon that would offer massive results. Nobel Prize–winning economist James Tobin proposed a 0.5 percent tax on foreign exchange transactions that whirl trillions of dollars around the planet. The tax would inhibit nothing but could be used to resurrect poor nations by easing their odious and crippling debts; it could finance the operations of the United Nations and its agencies focusing on universal literacy, clean water, and topsoil-saving agriculture. It could encourage the new wave of democracy, those Non-Governmental Organizations (NGOs) that bring local people-power to local problems.

No deity will come to save this gifted and generous earth. It's a challenge for humans not for gods. New heavens and a new earth are within our reach. The hour is late; some damage is irremediable. But it is not too late to start reversals. Old Deuteronomy put it to us, telling us the choices before us are for life or for death and begging us to choose life for the sake of our children (Deut. 30:19).

From Dilmun to Genesis

Human intelligence is blessed and cursed with a sense of possibility. The *might be* is an uncomfortable spur under our complacency.

Dreams of the paradise that might be haunt us and taunt us. This tension finds its way into print in one of the oldest written languages on earth, the Sumerian *cuneiform*. Their dreamers dreamed a dream of paradise, called Dilmun, which continued to echo in surrounding cultures long after Sumer ceased to exist. Dilmun was a place without disease, hunger, war, or sorrow. All expected conflicts were no more in this "pure place." Lions did not kill, wolves did not attack lambs, and grain-devouring boars were not known. Their music is free of dirge and lamentation. Sumerian writings show that there were troubles in this early third-century BCE society. Inequality in the distributions of resources was there and workers were exploited and enslaved. There are even hints of male dominance over women. And yet there was Dilmun, summoning their imaginations to peace and paradise right here on earth. Paradise stories are ethical challenges.

Dilmun was seen as nearby but not within the precincts of Sumer. It was, in other words, a beacon of possibilities not yet achieved, but out there.[32] It was poetry, not geography or history, and it echoes still in the Genesis story of paradise. Literal-minded folk have often taken the Genesis paradise story as fact and have done digs to see if there are remnants of this paradise somewhere between the Tigris and Euphrates rivers—a sorry witness to our metaphor-crushing dullness. There are enough hints in the Genesis story to make the point that this is myth, not facticity. The trees are not oak or elm but trees of life and of the knowledge of good and evil, serpents talk, and angels staff the gates to this paradise. This is Dilmun poetically calling out.

Dilmun and Genesis are at one with Herbert Marcuse's enigma: "That which is cannot be true." Our present debased existence is not definitive; it is not the fulfillment of the truth of which we are capable. John's epistle stands with Marcuse: "what we shall be has not yet been disclosed" (1 John 3:2). The realistic hopes and hungers of Dilmun and Genesis also resonate in biblical scholar Gerd Theissen when he suggests we call off the search for the "missing link" between apes and true humanity. Says Theissen, we are that missing link.[33] True humanity could not be marked by pogroms, Inquisitions, slavery, and ecocide; true humanity could not have polysaturated wealth of the few coexisting with excruciating poverty of the many. True humanity could not substitute kill-power for reasoning and diplomacy. Dilmun and Genesis and all their cousins in human mythic poetry insist that history is malleable, not cyclic. Vertical lines can take off in new directions.

There are possibilities, but possibilities are not certainties. What is certain is that if current trends continue, we will certainly not. There is nothing more practical or necessary or contemporary than the dreams of Dilmun and Genesis because we, as a species, can be crushed, in the suicide of small expectations. Can a species with stunted imagination arrange a marriage between *homo faber* and *homo somnians*, between the maker and the dreamer?

The jury is very much still out.

EPILOGUE

The God Loss

It is easy to sympathize with Mary Magdalene who stood weeping at the empty tomb. When asked why she was weeping she said, "They have taken my Lord away, and I do not know where they have laid him" (John 20:13). That reaction could greet this book of mine. Response could vary from grief to anger. Good friends and some former students may feel the hurt of disappointment. Yet it is the role of true scholars not to please but to probe, to follow the truth wherever it draws them, to share their findings, and await critique. That is the heat in the scholarly kitchen and those who work there must sweat it out, keep listening, and keep moving.

And yet, not all are disturbed when the "God" hypothesis is challenged. Polls in the United States show around one in four Americans to be in the "atheist/agnostic" category. Anonymous surveys on the first day of my recent classes at Marquette, a Jesuit Catholic university, show an even higher number in that category. Polls cast in terms of *theism vs. nontheism* can be deceptive since they leave out what may be the most important category, a category not easily captured in the linguistic confines of polling. *Indifference.* It has been said that "God" is not an operative category in the faculty lounges of the Ivy League. But even beyond those elite settings, in the quotidian transactions of many modern folks, "God" is no longer a pulsing presence. At best, "God" is regularly reduced to a rhetorical flourish.

It should be acknowledged, however, that for many believers—if they accept the arguments against the existence of a personal divine being, an invisible friend whom you can talk to and call on in emergencies—the sense of loss can be horrific. Ominous questions rise. Without belief in a personal deity who rewards and punishes according to our deserts, is morality not undone? Is "God" not the bulwark that stands between us and social chaos? If "God" is but a metaphor, and not the last word in law enforcement, what motivates people to do good and avoid evil? And if there is no afterlife where evil is punished and virtue rewarded, is life not rendered meaningless?

I believe the answer to all those questions is an emphatic *no*. God-talk is ambivalent, inspiring both atrocities and heroic works. It remains a matter of dispute whether theism in human history has done more good or harm. But the dispute hardly matters because there is always more to god-talk than the gods that we conjure. Deeper than hypotheses about "God" is the critical urgency to respond positively and creatively to the marvel that is life. The word "God" is lubricious and humanity has never agreed on its meaning. Human moral progress never depended on the shifting sands of orthodoxy nor did it rest on the marsh of unstable god-talk.

One can profit from the poetry of early Israel in its polytheistic period without embracing polytheism. Biblical disarray and confusion about afterlife in some parallel universe does not destroy the poetic brilliance of that complex classic. Many scholars think Jesus was totally mixed-up about the impending consummation of history, which he thought would happen during the lifetime of his listeners. Does Jesus' error strip the inspiring beauty of the Sermon on the Mount or undercut that literary gem with all its enduringly relevant Hebraic imagery? Paul, a major shaper of the Christian story, looked forward with confidence to lots of folks exiting their graves to meet the returning Jesus "in the air." Smile, if you will, but don't pass over all that fell from his gifted pen. No mind in any age—ancient, modern, or postmodern—is free of mythic shackles, but good thinking and inspiration are there like ores awaiting mining.

A theologian friend who read my manuscript is in somewhat reluctant agreement with the case I made but she chided me saying how it used to be exhilarating to wake and see the special glory of *Der Morgensonnenschein*, to feel invigorated by a sleep that "unravels care," and to say in the face of it all "Thank you, God!" The splendor of such a moment must not be lost. Gratitude is the beginning of all virtue. It is so much more important than an imagined personalized deity. Gratitude to be part of the grand natural miracle of life in its insistent, still unfolding mysterious splendor. Great as our minds are we cannot fathom all of the wonder that is our home, but gratitude poetically and joyfully expressed is a sweet and urgent duty. God-talk is never emptiness. It is rich in symbolic power. When we realize that "God" is not dead, that "God" as a person was never alive, our need of symbols does not die. Culture is a clash of symbols. The quest for a global ethic is a quest for new symbols and for old symbols now better understood. Symbols undergird choice and by our choices we live or die.

We are a spoiled species that seems hell-bent on wrecking the earth that cradles us and we are well on in that demonic suicidal project. It is an alluring temptation for the likes of us to imagine a divine superbeing with parental passions who is both omnipotent and all merciful (*omnipotens et misericors dominus*) who will make everything right "on earth as it is in heaven."

Such delusions are typical of adolescence. And adolescent is what we are. Maturity with a developed sense of responsibility has not yet happened in the social production we bless with undeserved encomia like "civilization" and "progress" and "modernity" and "development." Remember Gandhi's witticism when he was asked: "What do you think of Western civilization?" He replied: "That would be a wonderful idea!" His cynicism applies to East as well as West. As one scholar from India told me: "We are making the same mistakes that you did but we are doing it faster." Along with their own human nature the Indians, Chinese, et al. have us to thank. Our most successfully "developed" Western exports are parasitic consumption and oligarchical greed.

The symbol of a "God" as an indulgent parent who will clean up the mess left by our profligacy is a bad symbol. It deserves to die. Better symbols beckon to us. Among other places, they are there in the Bible. Putting the Bible's jumbled theism aside, there is a trove of power-making symbols there, symbols of a humanity that can level mountains and raise valleys, break chains and part waters, a humanity empowered by the courage to start out into a desert of uncharted healing possibilities. The symbols of resurrection and transfiguration were not events but poetic envisionings of human potential to make "a new heaven and a new earth," to break the grip of what seemed inexorable fate . . . to see paradise not as lost but as awaiting our discovery. These poetic symbols have no need of a supernal superbeing who is "the way, the truth, and the life." In us evolution flowered into thought and creativity. It is for us to find "the way," embrace "truth"—whether hard or exhilarating—and serve "life" as no species in the rest of nature can do.

NOTES

Chapter 1

1. Rita Nakashima Brock and Rebecca Ann Parker, *Saving Paradise: How Christianity Traded Love of This World for Crucifixion and Empire* (Boston: Beacon, 2008), xx.
2. Catherine Keller, *On the Mystery* (Minneapolis, MN: Fortress, 2008), xi.
3. Karen Armstrong, *A History of God: The 4000-Year Quest of Judaism, Christianity, and Islam* (New York: Ballantine Books, 1993), xix–xx. On the Enuma Elish of the Babylonians, "the epic poem which celebrated the victory of the gods over chaos," ibid., 7.
4. Karl Marx and Friedrich Engels, *Marx and Engels: Selected Words in Two Volumes* (Moscow: Foreign Languages Publishing House, 1958), I:138.
5. V. I. Lenin, *State and Revolution* (New York: International Publishers, 1932), 38.
6. Elaine Pagels, *Adam, Eve, and the Serpent* (New York: Random House, 1988), xxiii–xxiv.
7. Thomas Cahill, *The Gifts of the Jews: How a Tribe of Desert Nomads Changed the Way Everyone Thinks and Feels* (New York: Anchor Books: Doubleday, 1998), 3, 5.

8. Chun-Fang Yu, in *Visions of a New Earth: Religious Perspectives on Population, Consumption, and Ecology*, ed. Harold Coward and Daniel C. Maguire (Albany: State University of New York Press, 2000), 162.
9. Ibid.
10. Daniel C. Maguire, *Ethics: A Complete Method for Moral Choice* (Minneapolis, MN: Fortress, 2010), 29–50. See *Visions of a New Earth: Religious Perspectives on Population, Consumption, and Ecology*, ed. Harold Coward and Daniel C. Maguire (Albany, NY: State University of New York Press, 2000), 1–7.
11. Wing-tsit Chan, *A Source Book in Chinese Philosophy* (Princeton, NJ: Princeton University Press, 1963), 497–499.

Chapter 2

1. Catherine Bell, "Modernism and Postmodernism in the Study of Religion," *Religious Studies Review* 22.3 (July 1996): 179.
2. Robert Cummings Neville, "Religious Studies and the Theological Studies: AAR 1992 Presidential Address," in *Journal of the American Academy of Religion* 51 (1993): 185.
3. Wilfred Cantwell Smith, *The Meaning and End of Religion* (New York: New American Library, 1962), 21.
4. J. W. Bowker, "Information Process, Systemic Behavior, and the Study of Religion," *Zygon* 2: 361.
5. On the foundational moral experience, which is also the foundational religious experience in my use of the term, see Daniel C. Maguire, *Ethics: A Complete Method for Moral Choice* (Minneapolis, MN: Fortress, 2010), 29–50.
6. Augustine, *Sermo* 52, c. 6, n. 16.
7. Thomas Aquinas, *Quaestio Disputata de Spiritualibus Creaturis 11, ad 3*.
8. Thomas Aquinas, *Summa Theologiae*, I, q. 3. *Quia de Deo scire non possumus quid sit, sed quid non sit, non possumus considerare de Deo quomodo sit, sed potius quomodo non sit.* Thomas turns to analogy to salvage some knowledge of "God" but analogy only works between comprehensibles, not between a comprehensible and an incomprehensible of whom *scire non possumus quid sit*.

9. Elizabeth A. Johnson, *She Who Is: The Mystery of God in Feminist Theological Discourse* (New York: Crossroad, 1993), 7, 109.
10. Karen Armstrong, *A History of God: The 4000-Year Quest of Judaism, Christianity, and Islam* (New York: Ballantine Books, 1994), xx.
11. Denys the Areopagite, *The Divine Names* II, 7; VII, 3, XIII, 3.
12. Duns Scotus Erigena, *Periphesean, Migne Patres Latini, 426 C–D.*
13. Hans Urs von Balthasar, "The Unknown God," in *The von Balthasar Reader*, ed. Medard Kehl and Werner Loser, trans. Robert Daly and Fred Lawrence (New York: Crossroad, 1982), 186.
14. Cynthia Crysdale and Neil Ormerod, *Creator God, Evolving World* (Minneapolis, MN: Fortress, 2012), xii.
15. Humphrey Palmer, *Analogy* (London: Macmillan, 1978), xv.
16. Johnson, *She Who Is*, 110.
17. Robert Wright, *The Evolution of God* (New York: Little, Brown, 2009), 88.
18. Ibid., 101.
19. Jack Nelson-Pallmeyer, *Is Religion Killing Us?: Violence in the Bible and the Quran* (New York: Continuum, 2003), 28.
20. Jack Miles, *God: A Biography* (New York: Knopf, 1995), 20.
21. Armstrong, *History of God*, 23.
22. Nelson-Pallmeyer, *Is Religion Killing Us?* 60.
23. Regina M. Schwartz, *The Curse of Cain: The Violent Legacy of Monotheism*, (Chicago: University of Chicago Press, 1997), 77.
24. Henricus Denzinger, *Enchiridion Symbolorum: Definitionum et Declarationum De Rebus Fidei et Morum* (Freiburg, Germany: Herder, 1953, 29 Edition), #1784.
25. Douglas Johnston and Cynthia Sampson, ed., *Religion, The Missing Dimension of Statecraft* (New York: Oxford University Press, 1994).
26. John F. Haught, *What Is God?: How to Think About the Divine* (New York/Mahwah: Paulist, 1988), 6–7.
27. Ibid., 8.
28. Gordon D. Kaufman, "On Thinking of God as Serendipitous Creativity," *Journal of the American Academy of Religion*, vol. 69, no. 2 (June 2001): 413.
29. John Shelby Spong, *A New Christianity for a New World: Why*

Traditional Faith Is Dying and How a New Faith Is Being Born (San Francisco: HarperCollins, 2001), 63–64.

30. Ibid.
31. Ibid., 57.
32. Ibid., 57–77.
33. Ibid., 73.
34. Ibid., 191.
35. Ibid., 193.
36. Thomas Cahill, *The Gifts of the Jews: How a Tribe of Desert Nomads Changed the Way Everyone Thinks and Feels* (New York: Anchor Books: Doubleday, 1998), 250.
37. Gary Gutting, "On Being Catholic," *New York Times* (March 31, 2013). See www.@nytimes.com/opinionator, *The Stone*, for his fuller statement on what being a Catholic means to him.
38. Garry Wills, *Why Priests? A Failed Tradition* (New York: Viking, 2013), 258.
39. Robert W. Funk, *Honest to Jesus* (San Francisco: HarperCollins, 1996) 42, 305–306.

Chapter 3

1. Arnold J. Toynbee, *Change and Habit: The Challenge of Our Time* (New York: Oxford University Press, 1966), 106.
2. Ibid.
3. Ibid., 106–107.
4. Ibid., 112.
5. Leonard Shlain, *The Alphabet Versus the Goddess: The Conflict Between Word and Image* (New York: Viking, 1999), 6.
6. Ibid.
7. Ignatius Jesudasan, *Religion as Metaphor for Ethno-Ethical Identity* (Milwaukee, WI: Marquette University Press, 2011), 13.
8. Ibid., 55.
9. Jurgen Moltmann, "The Cross as Military Symbol for Sacrifice," in *Cross Examination: Readings on the Meaning of the Cross Today*, ed. Marit Trelstad (Minneapolis, MN: Fortress, 2006), 261.
10. Catherine Keller, *On the Mystery: Discerning God in Process* (Minneapolis, MN: Fortress, 2008), 32.

11. Rosemary Radford Ruether, *Sexism and God-Talk* (Boston: Beacon, 1993), 56.
12. Arnold J. Toynbee, *A Study of History* (New York: Oxford University Press, 1963), 7B: 718.
13. Dennis Nineham, *The Use and Abuse of the Bible* (London: Macmillan, 1975), 44.
14. Ibid., 200.
15. Roland J. Teske, S. J., "The Aim of Augustine's Proof That God Truly Is," *International Philosophical Quarterly*, 26:3 (September 1986): 253–255.
16. Ibid., 258.
17. Tertullian, *Adversus Prax., 7,* in Teske, "The Aim of Augustine's Proof," 255.
18. Dennis Nineham, *Christianity Mediaeval and Modern* (London: SCM Press, 1993), 49.
19. Ibid., 138.
20. Ibid., 93–94.
21. Ibid., 96.
22. Ibid., 86.
23. Ibid., 102.
24. Ibid., 80.
25. David R. Loy, "The Religion of the Market," in *Visions of a New Earth: Religious Perspectives on Population, Consumption, and Ecology*, ed. Harold Coward and Daniel C. Maguire (Albany, NY: State University of New York Press, 2000), 15–16.

Chapter 4

1. Karen Armstrong, *A History of God: The 4000-Year Quest of Judaism, Christianity, and Islam* (New York: Ballantine Books, 1994), 4.
2. Edward O. Wilson, *The Future of Life* (New York: Alfred A. Knopf, 2002), 3.
3. Carl Sagan, in *The Varieties of Scientific Experience: A Personal View of the Search for God*, ed. Ann Druyan (New York: Penguin, 2006), 28–29.
4. Ibid., 20.
5. See David Leeming with Margaret Leeming, *A Dictionary of Creation Myths* (New York: Oxford University Press, 1994).

6. Jacob K. Olupona, "African Religions and the Global Issues of Population Consumption, and Ecology," in *Visions of a New Earth: Religious Perspectives on Population, Consumption, and Ecology*, ed. Harold Coward and Daniel C. Maguire (Albany, NY: State University of New York Press, 2000), 183–191.
7. Steven Hawking, *A Brief History of Time: From the Big Bang to Black Holes* (New York: Bantam Books, 1988), 50.
8. Pope Pius XII, "The Proofs for the Existence of God in the Light of Modern Natural Science," reprinted as "Modern Science and the Existence of God," *Catholic Mind* 49 (1972): 182–192.
9. Victor Stenger, "Cosmic Evidence," in Christopher Hitchens, *The Portable Atheist* (Philadelphia: Da Capo Press/Perseus Books Group, 2007), 317.
10. Ibid., 321.
11. Carl Sagan, "Introduction," in Steven Hawking, *A Brief History of Time: From the Big Bang to Black Holes* (New York: Bantam Books, 1988), x.
12. Thomas Aquinas, *Summa Theologiae*, I, q. 2, a.3.
13. Richard Dawkins, *The God Delusion* (Boston, New York: Houghton Mifflin, 2008), 102.
14. Ibid., 141.
15. Sam Harris, *The End of Faith: Religion, Terror, and the Future of Reason* (New York: Norton, 2005), 129.
16. Ibid., 131.
17. G. K. Chesterton, *Lunacy and Letters*, ed. Dorothy Collins (New York: Sheed and Ward, 1958), 97.
18. Wilson, *Future of Life*, 131.
19. Dawkins, *God Delusion*, 145.
20. Charles Birch and John Cobb, *The Liberation of Life: From the Cell to the Community* (Denton, TX: Environmental Ethics Books, 1990), 45.
21. Dawkins, *God Delusion*, 147–148.
22. Ibid., 153.
23. Sagan, *Varieties of Scientific Experience*, 122.
24. Neil Shubin, *Your Inner Fish: A Journey into the 3.5 Billion-Year History of the Human Body* (New York: Random House, First Vintage Books, 2009), 184–185.

25. Larry L. Rasmussen, *Earth-Honoring Faith* (New York and London: Oxford University Press, 2013), 13.
26. Sagan, *Varieties of Scientific Experience*, 28, 115, 117–118, 125.
27. Ibid., 28–30.

Chapter 5

1. Robert W. Funk, *Honest to Jesus: Jesus for a New Millennium* (San Francisco: HarperCollins, 1996), 31.
2. Albert Nolan, *Jesus Before Christianity* (Maryknoll, NY: Orbis, 1978), 38; E. P. Sanders, *Jesus and Judaism* (Minneapolis: Fortress, 1985), 208.
3. Joseph A. Grassi, *God Makes Me Laugh: A New Approach to Luke* (Wilmington, DE: Michael Glazier, 1986), 35.
4. Anselm, *Cur Deus Homo?* Book 2, Chapter 9 (407C).
5. Garry Wills, *Why Priests? A Failed Tradition* (New York: Viking, 2013), 187, n. 24.
6. Jane Schaberg, *The Illegitimacy of Jesus: A Feminist Theological Interpretation of the Infancy Narratives* (San Francisco: Harper & Row, 1987), 1–5.
7. Hans Kung, *Christianity: Essence, History and Future* (New York: Continuum, 1995), 19.
8. Ibid., 25.
9. Walter Brueggemann, *David's Truth* (Minneapolis, MN: Fortress, 1985), 13.
10. William E. Phipps, *Was Jesus Married?* (New York: Harper & Row, 1970), 13.
11. John Schlaginhaufen, in *Luther's Works*, ed. H. T. Llehman (Philadelphia, 1957), 54, 154, Table Talk, no. 1472.
12. Phipps, *Was Jesus Married?*, 12.
13. Funk, *Honest to Jesus*, 44.
14. Robin R. Meyers, *Saving Jesus from the Church: How to Stop Worshiping Christ and Start Following Jesus* (San Francisco: HarperCollins, 2009), 71.
15. Funk, *Honest to Jesus*, 44.
16. Leonard Shlain, *The Alphabet Versus the Goddess: The Conflict Between Word and Image* (New York: Viking, 1999), 266.

17. It was Irish theologian Paul Surlis who first directed me to the prevalent docetism of traditional Christian piety.
18. Meyers, *Saving Jesus*, 53.
19. Marcus J. Borg has argued that the view that Jesus expected the end of history imminently became "the image of the historical Jesus which has dominated Jesus scholarship in this century." If Jesus were so deluded, then his relevance to how we live on earth to build up "the kingdom of God" today is cut short since if the end were nigh, Jesus could care little about the subsequent unfolding of human life on earth. See Borg, "A Temperate Case for a Non-eschatological Jesus," *Forum* 2 (September 1986): 81. See also Werner Georg Kummel, "Eschatological Expectation in the Proclamation of Jesus," in *The Kingdom of God*, ed. Bruce Chilton (Minneapolis, MN: Fortress, 1984), 36–51.
20. Robert W. Funk does not think Jesus thought the world was going to end immediately, unlike John the Baptist. He did not institute a Eucharist or found a church. Funk, *Honest to Jesus*, 41–42, 34.
21. Kung, *Christianity*, 77.
22. Walter Ullmann, *The Growth of Papal Government in the Middle Ages* (London: Methuen, 1955), 21.
23. John Dominic Crossan, *Jesus: A Revolutionary Biography* (San Francisco: HarperCollins, 1994), 25–26.
24. Pinchas Lapide, *The Sermon on the Mount: Utopia or Program for Action?* (Maryknoll, NY: Orbis, 1986), 9–10.
25. Kung, *Christianity*, 103.
26. Dennis Nineham, *The Use and Abuse of the Bible* (San Francisco: Harper & Row, 1976), 164.
27. Ibid., 155–166.
28. Elaine Pagels, *Beyond Belief: The Secret Gospel of Thomas* (New York: Random House, 2005), 58–59.
29. Pagels credits Irenaeus with shaping the "almost mathematical equation, in which God = Word = Jesus Christ. It was this "bold interpretation that came virtually to define orthodoxy," ibid., 151. Pagels notes the dominant influence of John's higher Christology. The Gospel of Thomas, which did not prevail or get into the canon, had a different view of Jesus' status and being. "If

Matthew, Mark, and Luke had been joined with the Gospel of Thomas, instead of with John, for example, or had both John and Thomas been included in the New Testament canon, Christians probably would have read the first three gospels quite differently," ibid., 38.

30. Kung, *Christianity,* 93, 95.
31. A. N. Wilson, *Jesus: A Life* (New York: Fawcett Columbine, 1992), 57.
32. E. P. Sanders, *Jesus and Judaism* (Minneapolis, MN: Fortress, 1983), 321.
33. Robert Funk writes: "Constantine saw to it that the vote was unanimous by banishing the bishops who did not put their signatures to the creed." *Honest to Jesus,* 37.
34. Rita Nakashima Brock and Rebecca Ann Parker, *Saving Paradise: How Christianity Traded Love of This World for Crucifixion and Empire* (Boston: Beacon, 2008), 106–110.

Chapter 6

1. E. P. Sanders, *Jesus and Judaism* (Minneapolis, MN: Fortress, 1985), 320.
2. A. N. Wilson, *Jesus: A Life* (New York: Fawcett Columbine, 1992), 19.
3. John Dominic Crossan, *Jesus: A Revolutionary Biography* (San Francisco: HarperCollins, 1994), 27.
4. Leonard Shlain, *The Alphabet versus the Goddess: The Conflict between Word and Image* (New York: Viking, 1998), 254.
5. Anthony E. Harvey, quoted in Sanders, *Jesus and Judaism,* 6.
6. Sanders, *Jesus and Judaism,* 325.
7. Hans Kung, *Christianity: Essence, History and Future* (New York: Continuum, 1995), 68.
8. Ibid., 68–69.
9. Shlain, *The Alphabet versus the Goddess,* 220.
10. Marcus J. Borg, "A Temperate Case for a Non-Eschatological Jesus," *Forum* 2 (September 1986): 81; *Jesus: A New Vision* (San Francisco: HarperCollins, 1987), 14, 20, n. 25.

11. Kung, *Christianity*, 77–78.
12. Elisabeth Schussler Fiorenza, *In Memory of Her: A Feminist Theological Reconstruction of Christian Origins* (New York: Crossroads,1983), 121.
13. Kung, *Christianity*, 83–84.
14. Augustine, Sermon 227. See Garry Wills, *Why Priests? A Failed Tradition* (New York: Viking, 2013), 16, 49–50, 55–56, 58.
15. Wills, *Why Priests?*, 7.
16. Elaine Pagels, *Beyond Belief: The Secret Gospel of Thomas* (New York: Random House, 2005), 19.
17. Robin R. Meyers, *Saving Jesus from the Church: How to Stop Worshiping Christ and Start Following Jesus* (San Francisco: HarperCollins, 2009), 26.
18. "Mithraism," in the *Oxford Dictionary of the Christian Church*, eds. F. L. Cross and E. A. Livingstone (New York and London: Oxford University Press, 1974), 924.
19. Abraham J. Heschel, *The Prophets* (Philadelphia: Jewish Publication Society of America, 1962), 327; Arnold Toynbee, *A Study of History* (New York: Oxford University Press, 1963), 7 B: 357–359; Rosemary Radford Ruether, *Sexism and God-Talk* (Boston: Beacon, 1983), 48–52; Yves Bonnefoy, *Mythologies* (Chicago: University of Chicago Press, 1991), I: 661–663.
20. The more scholars dig into history the more they undermine claims of originality in the Hebrew and Christian scriptures and tradition. For example, in Sumerian mythology, we see Ut-napishtim who became the model for Noah and the flood. Ut-napishtim was given guidance to save his family and a remnant of all living things by building an ark when the gods decided to destroy the human race. Thomas Cahill, *The Gifts of the Jews: How a Tribe of Desert Nomads Changed the Way Everyone Thinks and Feels the Gifts of the Jews* (New York: Doubleday Anchor Book, 1998), 34.
21. Wilson, *Jesus: A Life*, x–xi, xvi, 21, 50, 56, 161, 197–198, 160–161.
22. Shlain, *The Alphabet versus the Goddess*, 225.
23. Ibid., 224.
24. Crossan, *Jesus*, xi, 160–161. Crossan sees Easter as not a day but a metaphor for the perdurance of the Jesus movement even after his horrible death. Claiming to have seen Jesus resurrected was

a way of claiming authority in the forming movement. On the utter shame of crucifixion and the delay of burial until the wild beasts and birds of prey had their way with the body, see Martin Hengel, *Crucifixion in the Ancient World and the Folly of the Message of the Cross* (Minneapolis, MN: Fortress, 1977).

25. Sanders, *Jesus and Judaism*, 317.
26. Ibid., 295.
27. Ibid., 326.
28. Ibid., 306.
29. Quoted in *God and Capitalism: A Prophetic Critique of Market Economy*, eds. J. Mark Thomas and Vernon Visick (Madison, WI: A-R Editions, 1991), 18.
30. Crossan, *Jesus*, 25. Crossan says 95 to 97 percent of the Jewish state was illiterate at the time of Jesus. Though well versed in the narratives of his oral culture, he was probably illiterate, too. Luke 2:41–52, where Jesus is portrayed as skilled in biblical texts, is dismissed by Crossan as "Lukan propaganda," 26.
31. Shlain, *The Alphabet versus the Goddess*, 241.
32. "Circumincession" in *Oxford Dictionary of the Christian Church*, eds. F. L. Cross and E. A. Livingstone (London: Oxford University Press, 1974), 295.
33. See Crossan, *The Greatest Prayer: Rediscovering the Revolutionary Message of the Lord's Prayer* (San Francisco: HarperCollins, 2010).
34. Robin Meyers, *Saving Jesus*, 8.
35. Crossan, *Greatest Prayer*, 2.
36. John Dominic Crossan and Jonathan L. Reed, *In Search of Paul* (San Francisco: Harper, 2004), 11.
37. Sanders, *Jesus and Judaism*, 295.
38. Suetonius, *Claudius*, xxv.
39. Joerg Rieger, *Christ and Empire* (Minneapolis, MN: Fortress, 2007), 31.
40. Walter Wink, *Engaging the Powers: Discernment and Resistance in a World of Domination* (Minneapolis, MN: Fortress, 1992), 175.
41. Ibid.
42. Gandhi in *Harijan*, March 10, 1946, cited by Mark Juergensmeyer, *Fighting with Gandhi* (San Francisco: Harper & Row, 1984), 43.
43. Ibid.

Chapter 7

1. See Eduardo Galeano, *Open Veins of Latin America: Five Centuries of the Pillage of a Continent* (New York: Monthly Review Press, 1997).
2. Alfred North Whitehead, *Process and Reality: An Essay in Cosmology* (New York: Macmillan, 1929), 404.
3. Norman K. Gottwald, *The Tribes of Yahweh: A Sociology of the Religion of Liberated Israel 1250–1050 B.C.E.* (Maryknoll, NY: Orbis, 1979), 615.
4. Ibid.
5. Ibid., 613.
6. Ibid., 613–614.
7. Ibid., 593.
8. A. N. Wilson, *Jesus: A Life* (New York: Fawcett Columbine, 1992), 38.
9. Hans Kung, *Christianity: Essence, History and Future* (New York: Continuum, 1995), 93. For Paul, Jesus is not, as later orthodoxy would insist, "personified pre-existent wisdom."
10. Ibid., 113.
11. Robert Bruce McLaren, *Christian Ethics: Foundations and Practice* (Englewood Cliffs, NJ: Prentice Hall, 1994), 14–18.
12. See Adrian Hastings, ed., *The Oxford Companion to Christian Thought* (London: Oxford University Press, 2000), 51–52.
13. Jurgen Moltmann, in *Cross Examinations: Readings on the Meaning of the Cross Today*, ed. Marit Trelstad (Minneapolis, MN: Fortress, 2006), 260.
14. Ibid., 261.
15. Origen, *Against Celsus* (Contra Celsum), 8, 74.
16. Tertullian, *Idolatry* (De Idolotria), XIX.
17. Lactantius, *The Divine Institutes, (Divinarum institutionum libre)*, VI, xx, 15–16.
18. Roland Bainton, *Christian Attitudes toward War and Peace: A Historical Survey and Critical Re-Evaluation* (New York: Abingdon, 1960), 73.
19. Eusebius, *Life of Constantine* (*Vita Constantini*), 1, 24.
20. Lactantius, *The Divine Institutes*, VII, 26.
21. Stanley Windass, *Christianity versus Violence: A Social and Historical*

Study of War and Christianity (London: Sheed and Ward, 1964), 43.
22. Augustine, *Epist. 138*, n. 14.
23. Quoted in *Bainton, Christian Attitudes*, 110.
24. Ibid., 110.
25. Windass, *Christianity versus Violence*, 43.
26. Bainton, *Christian Attitudes*, 111–112.
27. Quoted in *Bainton, Christian Attitudes*, 112–113.
28. Alice Beck Kehoe, *Militant Christianity: An Anthropological History* (New York: Palgrave Macmillan, 2012), 1.
29. Karen Armstrong, *A History of God* (New York: Ballantine Books, 1993), 358.
30. Chris Hedges, *What Every Person Should Know About War* (New York: Free Press, 2003), 1.
31. Erich Fromm, *The Anatomy of Human Destructiveness* (New York: Holt, Rinehart and Winston, 1973), 105.

Chapter 8

1. John Dewey, in Corliss Lamont, *The Illusion of Immortality, Fifth Edition* (New York: Continuum, 1990), xi.
2. William R. LaFleur, *Liquid Life: Abortion and Buddhism in Japan* (Princeton, NJ: Princeton University Press, 1992), 26.
3. Ibid., 26–27.
4. David Loy, "The Karma of Women," in *Violence Against Women in Contemporary World Religions: Roots and Cures*, eds. Daniel C. Maguire and Sa'diyya Shaikh (Cleveland, OH: Pilgrim, 2007), 59.
5. Erich Fromm, *The Greatness and Limitations of Freud's Thought* (London: Sphere Books, 1982), 1, 3.
6. Robert Wright, *The Evolution of God* (New York: Little, Brown, 2009), 24.
7. Alan Richardson, ed., *A Theological Wordbook of the Bible* (New York: Macmillan, 1964), 33. Tertullian in his *De Corona,* PL., 2, 78 ff. said the Bible had no clear teaching on the subject of afterlife.
8. John Bowker, ed., *The Oxford Dictionary of World Religions* (New York: Oxford University Press, 1997), 417.
9. Dennis Nineham, *Christianity Mediaeval and Modern* (London: SCM Press, 1993), 133.

10. Jon Davies, *Death, Burial and Rebirth in the Religions of Antiquity* (London and New York: Routledge, 1999), 112.
11. Ibid., 111–112.
12. Nineham, *Christianity Mediaeval and Modern*, 139.
13. A. N. Wilson, *Jesus: A Life* (New York: Fawcett Columbine, 1992), 6.
14. Irenaeus, *Libros Quinque Adversus Haereses*, 2,32.4, cited in Elaine Pagels, *Beyond Belief: The Secret Gospel of Thomas* (New York: Random House, 2003), 7.
15. John Dominic Crossan, *Jesus: A Revolutionary Biography* (San Francisco: HarperCollins, 1994), 95.
16. Thomas Cahill, *The Gifts of the Jews: How a Tribe of Desert Nomads Changed the Way Everyone Thinks and Feels* (New York: Doubleday Anchor Books, 1998), 147.
17. Lucretius, *On the Nature of Things*, 235.
18. Ernest Becker, *The Denial of Death* (New York: Macmillan, 1973), 87.
19. Leonard Shlain, *The Alphabet versus the Goddess: The Conflict Between Word and Image* (New York: Viking, 1998), 28–29.
20. Rita Nakashima Brock and Rebecca Ann Parker, *Saving Paradise: How Christianity Traded Love of This World for Crucifixion and Empire* (Boston: Beacon, 2008), 72.
21. Paul got some support for this docking in space from the very poetic book of *Daniel*. Daniel dreamt that he saw "one like a man coming with the clouds of heaven; he approached the Ancient in Years and was presented to him. Sovereignty and glory and kingly power were given to him, so that all people and nations of every language should serve him, his sovereignty was to be an everlasting sovereignty which should not pass away" (Daniel 7:13–15).
22. De Visione Dei Beatifica et de Novissimis, Benedict XII, January 29, 1336, in Henry Denzinger, *Enchiridion Symbolorum* (Freiburg, Germany: Herder, 1953), 530.
23. Hal Lindsay, with C. C. Carlson, *The Late Great Planet Earth* (New York: Bantam Books, 1973), 99.
24. Nakashima Brock and Parker note that "the use of 'kingdom of the Heaven' in Matthew and 'heaven' in John carry a strong

this-worldly emphasis and describe how life should be on the earth . . ." *Saving Paradise*, 431, n. 6. J. E. Wright argues that the Greek and Roman cosmologies with a heaven above and an underworld below played into all this. It was background for the heaven for the good and hell for the bad.

25. J. Edward Wright, *The Early History of Heaven* (New York: Oxford University Press, 2000), 209.
26. Ibid., 211. There is also hope offered that "indescribably gorgeous virginal female beings exist in paradise to attend to the pious Muslim male's every physical and sexual desire." Ibid., 212. That is far from the sexless heaven that Jesus imagined.
27. Nineham, *Christianity Mediaeval and Modern*, 134. (The reference is to *Patres Latini*, 41, 745.)
28. Ibid., 135.
29. Nakashima Brock and Parker, *Saving Paradise*, 439, n. 5, 59.
30. Nineham, *Christianity Mediaeval and Modern*, 135.
31. Ibid., 138.
32. LaFleur, *Liquid Life*, 4–10.
33. Anne Wilson Schaef, *Women's Reality: An Emerging Female System in the White Male Society* (Minneapolis, MN: Winston, 1981), 142.
34. Charlotte Perkins Gilman, *His Religion and Hers* (New York: Century, 1923), 46–47.
35. Daniel C. Maguire and Larry L. Rasmussen, *Ethics for a Small Planet: New Horizons on Population, Consumption, and Ecology* (Albany, NY: State University of New York Press, 1998), 44–45.
36. Jared Diamond, *Guns, Germs, and Steel: The Fates of Human Societies* (New York: Norton, 1999), 28.
37. Ibid., 38.
38. Ibid., 39.

Chapter 9

1. Quoted in Larry L. Rasmussen, *Earth Community, Earth Ethics* (Maryknoll, NY: Orbis, 1996), 87, n. 40.
2. Jared Diamond, *Collapse: How Societies Choose to Fail or Succeed* (New York: Penguin, 2005), 6–7.

3. Stefan Rahmsdorf and Dim Coumou, "Increase of Extreme Events in a Warming World," *Proceedings of the National Academy of Sciences* 108, no. 44 (November 1, 2012): 1704–1709.
4. Diamond, *Collapse*, 6.
5. Edward O. Wilson, *The Future of Life*, (New York: Knopf, 2002), 129.
6. Carl Sagan, in *The Varieties of Scientific Experience: A Personal View of the Search for God*, ed. Ann Druyan (New York: Penguin, 2006), 214, 211.
7. Quoted in Goran Moller, *Ethics and the Life of Earth* (Leuven, Belgium: Peeters, 1998), 35.
8. Quoted in Elizabeth Kolbert, "Annals of Science: The Climate of Man—III," *New Yorker* (May 9, 2005): 57.
9. Harold F. Dorn, "World Population Growth: An International Dilemma," *Science* (January 26, 1962), reprinted in *Readings in Conservation Ecology*, ed. George W. Cox (New York: Appleton-Century-Crofts, 1969), 275.
10. Clive Ponting, *A Green History of the World: The Environment and the Collapse of Great Civilizations* (New York: Penguin, 1991), 254.
11. Ibid., 351.
12. See Daniel C. Maguire, *Ethics: A Complete Method for Moral Choice* (Minneapolis, MN: Fortress, 2010), 11–12.
13. Johannes Messner, *Social Ethics: Natural Law in the Western World*, rev. ed. (St. Louis and London: B. Herder, 1964), 705. Thomas is commenting on the *Second Book of Politics* of Aristotle.
14. U.S. Department of State, *Proceedings and Documents of the United Nations Monetary and Financial Conference*, Bretton Woods, New Hampshire, July 1–22, 1944, vol. 1, 790, as cited by Bruce Rich, *Mortgaging the Earth* (Boston: Beacon, 1994), 54–55.
15. David Korten says that economic globalization is nothing more than imperialism in new dress, a modern form of the imperialistic goal to transfer income from the middle and lower classes to the upper classes. David Korten, *When Corporations Rule the World* (West Hartford, CT: Kumarian, 1995), 28.
16. Lynn White Jr., "The Historical Roots of our Ecologic Crisis," *Science* 155 (March 10, 1967): 1203–1207. White had raised these issues twenty years earlier in "Natural Science and Naturalistic

Art in the Middle Ages," *American Historical Review* 52 (April 1947): 421–423.

17. Jack Nelson-Pallmeyer, *Is Religion Killing Us?* (New York: Continuum, 2003), xiv.
18. Ibid., xv.
19. Susan Solomon et al., "Irreversible Climate Change Due to Carbon Dioxide Emissions, *Proceedings of the National Academy of Science* 106, no. 6 (February 10, 2009): 1704–1709.
20. John Bellamy Foster and Brett Clark, "The Planetary Emergency," in *Monthly Review*, vol. 64, no. 7 (December 2012): 2.
21. Ibid.
22. Ibid.
23. Quoted ibid.
24. Thomas Kuhn, *The Structure of Scientific Revolution* (Chicago: University of Chicago Press, 1966), 91–92.
25. Clifford Geertz, "Religion in a Cultural System," in *The Religious Situation 1968*, ed. Donald R. Cutler (Boston: Beacon, 1968), 663, as cited in the discussion of John Shea, *Stories of God* (Chicago: Thomas More, 1978), 43.
26. Andrew Bacevich, "The End of (Military) History? The United States, Israel, and the Failure of the Western Way of War," accessed April 9, 2012, http://huffingtonpost.com/andres-bacevich/the-end-of-milit . . ..
27. Edward O. Wilson, *The Future of Life* (New York: Knopf, 2002), 189.

Chapter 10

1. Jacob Bronowski, *Science and Human Values* (New York: Harper & Row, 1965), 3–4.
2. Arthur Schopenhauer, *The Basis of Morality* (London: George Allen & Unwin, 1915), 6.
3. Amherst College, *Catalogue, 1895*, 32.
4. Douglas Sloan, "The Teaching of Ethics in the American Undergraduate Curriculum 1876–1976," in *Ethics Teaching in Higher Education*, eds. Daniel Callahan and Sissela Bok (New York: Plenum, 1980), 9.

5. As an example of this, see Michael Cronin, *The Science of Ethics* (New York: Benziger Brothers, 1917). Interestingly, Cronin was a clergyman doing ethics invoking God and religion. Even God had to be put under the mantle of science.
6. See Daniel C. Maguire, *Sacred Energies: When the World's Religions Sit Down to Talk About the Future of Life and the Plight of This Planet* (Minneapolis, MN: Fortress, 2000).
7. Jonathan Schell, *The Unconquerable World* (New York: Metropolitan Books, 2003), 366.
8. Ibid., 349.
9. Ibid., 370.
10. Quoted ibid., 366.
11. Richard Falk, "Why International Law Matters," *Nation* 276, no. 9 (March 10, 2003): 20.
12. Barbara Ehrenreich, *Blood Rites: Origins and History of the Passions of War* (New York: Holt, 1997), 177–178.
13. Medea Benjamin, *Drone Warfare: Killing by Remote Control* (New York: OR Books, 2012), 19.
14. Ibid.
15. Narrow secularists will miss a 2013 book from Oxford University Press on ecology. This volume merits the encomium *masterpiece*. It is entitled *Earth-Honoring Faith: Religious Ethics in a New Key*. The author, Larry L. Rasmussen, probes deeply and deftly into the roots of our ecological crisis, handling in novel ways the science, the social psychology, the commodification of value, and the partiality of most ecological analyses; he gives a critique of false religious and culturally ensconced ideas that have caused and augmented the ongoing collapse. However, those words in the title—"Faith" and "Religious"—will put this book on the Secularist's Index of Forbidden Books. The Vatican's old *Index Librorum Prohibitorum* was not unique but an example of commonplace myopic bias.
16. David Loy, "The Karma of Women," in *Violence against Women in Contemporary World Religions: Roots and Cures*, eds. Daniel C. Maguire and Sa'diyya Shaikh (Cleveland, OH: Pilgrim, 2007), 59.
17. See chapter 5, p. 138, for the specific quote from Erich Fromm, *The Greatness and Limitations of Freud's Thought* (London: Sphere Books, 1982), 1, 3.

18. Quoted in Larry L. Rasmussen, *Earth Community Earth Ethics* (Maryknoll, NY: Orbis, 1996), 87, n. 40.

Chapter 11

1. See Daniel C. Maguire, *The Moral Core of Judaism and Christianity* (Minneapolis, MN: Fortress Press, 1993), 70–77.
2. Norman K. Gottwald, *The Tribes of Yahweh: A Sociology of the Religion of Liberated Israel, 1250–1050 B.C.E.* (Maryknoll, NY: Orbis, 1979), 902.
3. Israel Finkelstein and Neil Asher Silberman, *The Bible Unearthed* (New York: Simon & Schuster, 2002), 118.
4. Robert Wright, *The Evolution of God* (New York: Little, Brown, 2009), 108–109.
5. Gottwald, *Tribes of Yahweh*, 490.
6. Ibid., 596.
7. Ibid., 614.
8. Gerhard E. Lenski, *Power and Privilege: A Theory of Social Stratification* (New York: McGraw-Hill, 1966), 267, 212–214, 219, 226–228. Lenski thinks a more complex model than the pyramid is needed to show the varying levels of distribution. Thus priests and merchants and artisans did better and even the peasants were better than the lowest tiers of the "unclean and degraded" and the "expendables," 284–285.
9. See Jan Dus, "Moses or Joshua? On the Problem of the Founder of the Israelite Religion," *Radical Religion* 2:2/3 (1975): 28.
10. George E. Mendenhall, *The Tenth Generation: The Origins of the Biblical Tradition* (Baltimore: Johns Hopkins University Press, 1973), 12.
11. Ibid., 216–217.
12. Ibid., 12.
13. See Dus, "Moses or Joshua?" 28.
14. Gottwald, *Tribes of Yahweh*, 615, 675.
15. Morton Smith, "Palestinian Judaism in the First Century," in *Israel: Its Role in Civilization*, ed. Moshe David (New York: Harper, 1956), 67–81.
16. Ibid., 81.

17. The Exodus story continues in the Christian gospels. Isaiah 40 was an application of the Exodus to the return from exile. It is bursting with hope of newness. And in one sense there are four, not three synoptic gospels for all four of them, early on, cite Isaiah 40 on finding a new way forward.
18. David Tracy, *The Analogical Imagination* (New York: Crossroad, 1981), 108.
19. Frank Kermode, *The Classic: Literary Images of Permanence and Change* (New York: Viking, 1975), 17–18.
20. Michel Foucault, *Power/Knowledge: Selected Interviews and Other Writings, 1972–1977* (New York: Pantheon Books, 1980), 81.
21. Herbert Marcuse, *One Dimensional Man: Studies in the Ideology of Advanced Industrial Society* (Boston: Beacon Press, 1966), 63.
22. Walter Brueggemann, *Journey to the Common Good* (Louisville, KY: Westminster John Knox, 2010), 91. My use of Brueggemann does not imply that he subscribes to my views on theism or life after death.
23. Ibid., 117–121.
24. Ibid., 38.
25. Ibid., 121.
26. Ibid., 3.
27. Susan George, "A Short History of Neoliberalism," in *The Other Davos: The Globalization of Resistance to the World Economic System*, eds. Francois Houtart and Francois Polet (London and New York: Zed Books, 2001), 10–11.
28. Joseph Stiglitz, "Inequality Is Holding Back the Recovery," *New York Times*, January 20, 2013, *Sunday Review*, 8.
29. See Mary Elizabeth Hobgood, *Dismantling Privilege: An Ethics of Accountability* (Cleveland, OH: Pilgrim, 2009).
30. Michael Zweig, "Six Points on Class," *Monthly Review*, vol. 58, no. 03 (July/August 2006), 2.

Chapter 12

1. Aristotle, *Nichomachean Ethics*, 1132 b. Aristotle puts it more cryptically saying, "it is by proportionate requital that the city holds together."

2. Thomas Aquinas, *Commentary on the Nichomachean Ethics of Aristotle*, 8, 9 #1648. Thomas says *justitia* consists in *communicatione*, and *commnicatio* is best rendered as sharing, rendering *commune* that which was *proprium*.
3. Michael Walzer, *Exodus and Revolution* (New York: Basic Books, 1985), 149.
4. Hannah Arendt, *The Human Condition* (Garden City, NY: Doubleday, 1959), 287–288.
5. Walter Brueggemann, *Journey to the Common Good* (Louisville, KY: Westminster John Knox, 2013), 38–39. Idem, *Revelation and Violence: A Study in Contextualization* (Milwaukee, WI: Marquette University, 1986), 14–20.
6. Eric Voegelin, *The New Science of Politics* (New York: Citadel Press, 1964), 100.
7. Karl Marx and Friedrich Engels, *Marx and Engels: Selected Words in Two Volumes* (Moscow: Foreign Languages Publishing House, 1958), I:138.
8. Douglas Meeks, *God the Economist* (Minneapolis: Fortress, 1989), 3.
9. T. R. Reid, *The Healing of America: A Global Quest for Better, Cheaper, and Fairer Health Care* (New York: Penguin, 2010), 1.
10. Ibid., 214.
11. Richard Hofstadter, *The American Political Tradition and the Men Who Made It* (New York: Vintage, 1954), vii.
12. Thomas Jefferson, to the Rev. James Madison, October 28, 1785, quoted in Y. Arieli, *Individualism and Nationalism in American Ideology* (Cambridge: Harvard University Press, 1964), 159.
13. Gerard E. Lenski, *Power and Privilege: A Theory of Social Stratification* (New York: McGraw-Hill, 1966), 274–275.
14. Abraham Heschel, *A Passion for Truth* (New York: Farrar, Straus, and Giroux, 1973), 259.
15. Brueggemann, *Journey*, 15–18.
16. Ibid., 44.
17. Ibid., 45–56.
18. Ibid., 55.
19. On the multiple forms of power operating in society, see Daniel C. Maguire, *Ethics: A Complete Method for Moral Choice* (Minneapolis, MN: Fortress, 2010), 88–90.

20. Abraham Heschel, *The Prophets* (Philadelphia: Jewish Publication Society of America, 1962), 166.
21. On the "policing paradigm" as the only legitimate form of military power, an idea enshrined in the United Nations Charter, see Daniel C. Maguire, *The Horrors We Bless: Rethinking the Just-War Legacy* (Minneapolis, MN: Fortress, 2007), 3–5.
22. Brueggemann, *Revelation and Violence*, 25–26.
23. Andrew Bacevich, "The End of (Military) History? The United States, Israel, and the Failure of the Western Way of War," *Huffington Post*, accessed April 9, 2012, http://www.huffingtonpost.com/andres-bacevich/the-end-of-milit. . . .
24. Herbert Marcuse, *One Dimensional Man: Studies in the Ideology of Advanced Industrial Society* (Boston: Beacon, 1966), 63.
25. Ibid., 123.
26. Franciscus Zorell, *Lexicon Graecum Novi Testamenti* (Paris: Letheilleux, 1931), 828–830.
27. Norman K. Gottwald, *The Tribes of Yahweh: A Sociology of the Religion of Liberated Israel, 1250–1050 B.C.E.* (Maryknoll, NY: Orbis, 1979), 485–489.
28. Walter Wink, *Jesus and Nonviolence: A Third Way* (Minneapolis, MN: Fortress, 2003), 52–53.
29. Jonathan Schell, *The Unconquerable World: Power, Nonviolence, and the Will of the People* (New York: Holt, 2003), 371.
30. Wangari Maathai, "All We Need Is Will," in *Can the Environment Be Saved Without a Radical New Approach to World Development?* (Geneva: CONGO Planning Committee for UNCED, 1992), 27.
31. David Korten, *When Corporations Rule the World* (West Hartford, CT: Kumarian, 1995), 303.
32. Rita Nakashima Brock and Rebecca Ann Parker, *Saving Paradise: How Christianity Traded Love of This World for Crucifixion and Empire* (Boston: Beacon, 2008), 4–8.
33. Gerd Theissen, *Biblical Faith: An Evolutionary Approach* (Minneapolis, MN: Fortress, 1985), 122.

SELECT ANNOTATED BIBLIOGRAPHY

The four parts of this book look at the existence of a personal deity, the deification of Jesus of Nazareth, continued living after death in an invisible parallel universe, and finally, the epic vision of what humanity and life on earth could be, a vision that has often been lost in the literalism of the dogmatic mélange.

Further Readings on the "God" Hypothesis

The discovery that we make the gods, and also that the gods do not make us or control our destiny, is richly illumined in historical studies. *The Evolution of God* by Robert Wright (Little, Brown, 2009) is a beautifully written account of the birth and the growth of the gods. It describes the slow birthing of biblical monotheism, and the invention of Christianity and Islam. And, in what is a special treat, the author demonstrates the compatibility of sound scholarship and wit.

Leonard Shlain is fascinated by the relationship between the disappearance of the goddesses and the invention of literacy. In *The Alphabet Versus the Goddess: The Conflict Between Word and Image*

(Viking, 1998), he treats the psychology and the history of the human proclivity to make, shape, and reshape our divinities.

Karen Armstrong's *A History of God: The 4,000 Year Quest of Judaism, Christianity and Islam* (Ballantine Books, 1993) delivers on the promise of its title. The book begins with the Jews' transforming pagan idols and their long trek to a kind of uneasy monotheism. Armstrong is especially helpful in understanding the "myth of Exodus" and the place it held in subsequent Jewish and Christian history.

Jack Miles makes a fine contribution to this learned chorus in *God: A Biography* (Alfred Knopf, 1995). He shows how "God" is a literary character that must be reckoned with, even if one does not believe in the personification of this god. He shows, too, that "God's" sudden sustained interest in morality came only after the Exodus story took hold.

Rosemary Radford Ruether, in *Gaia & God: An Ecofeminist Theology of Earth Healing* (Harper San Francisco, 1992), writes about how creation stories are also blueprints for social organization. She looks at the Babylonian, Hebrew, Greek, and Christian stories and addresses how these are supplanted by the creation story emerging from science—always with an eye to the ecological implications of these myths.

Among contemporary atheists, none is the match of Richard Dawkins. In *The God Delusion* (Houghton Mifflin Company, 2008), Dawkins brings science, wit, and sensitivity to the critique of theism. This is a rich work that leaves no relevant stone untouched in the does-a-personal-deity exist discussion. Dawkins had already shown that science can be written readably and he does it again here.

In what could be called "The Best of Sagan" regarding the interplay of gods and people, see Carl Sagan's *The Varieties of Scientific Experience: A Personal View of the Search for God*, (Penguin Press, 2006), edited by Ann Druyan. In 1985 Sagan was invited to give the Gifford Lecture in Scotland and in this book he treats not just the "God" hypothesis but also the ways in which science and religion could join in saving the planet. Among many things in this rich ensemble he argues that afterlife hopes can function as a substitute for the gritty work of justice.

Stephen Hawking, in *A Brief History of Time: From the Big Bang to Black Holes* (Bantam Books, 1988), addresses the truly foundational questions of how the universe began and why, and if it ends, how will that happen, and he raises the question of what need there could be of a personal deity in all that.

Historian Ludovic Kennedy wrote *All in the Mind: A Farewell to God* (Hodder & Stoughton, 1999). He traces out the journey of the Christian "God" and the challenges facing that god in history. He sees the Christian "God" as destined to take its humble place with the gods of Olympus and the Nile to be replaced eventually by poetry and the arts.

Stewart Guthrie sees religion as systematic anthropomorphism, the attribution of human characteristics to nonhuman things or events. He does this in his book *Faces in the Clouds: A New Theory of Religion* (Oxford University Press, 1993). He writes, not as a scholar of religion but as an anthropologist who observes the inevitability of anthropomorphizing in the creation of the gods.

Jesus: The Man and the Myths

Never in history has so much been written about someone of whom we know so little. The absence of solid facts has never deterred the endless flow of volumes pretending to detail the life of Jesus of Nazareth. Strong resistance has met the scholarly efforts to save Jesus from Christ, to pierce the myths and learn what little we can tentatively say about this man.

To get around Christ and find what you can of Jesus, a good start is John Dominic Crossan's *Jesus: A Revolutionary Biography* (Harper San Francisco, 1994). Crossan writes with the passion of an historian and moves through the legends, like the Christmas and Easter stories, to see what can more modestly and more honestly be claimed as truth. This is the *motif* of anything that bears the name of Crossan.

Sharing Crossan's relentless quest for objectivity in Jesus studies is his colleague Robert W. Funk. See particularly his *Honest to Jesus: Jesus for a New Millennium* (Harper San Francisco, 1996). Funk writes from a lifetime of study, gathering clues about this Jesus wherever they can be found. He finds enough to see Jesus as a radically challenging individual. Jesus' vision was daunting, says Funk, and Christians shied from it, neglecting the vision and elevating the visionary, turning the iconoclast into an icon. Funk touts the joys of being a senior scholar—less need to cower as one searches out discomfiting truths.

A. N. Wilson has written distinguished biographies and brought his studious skills to a biography of Jesus in *Jesus: A Life* (Fawcett Columbine, 1992). Wilson sees Jesus as a man who never claimed to be a god. Jesus could never have foreseen what Paul and John and the imaginative binges of subsequent councils would do to him, how endless ruminations about what he was would obscure the moral movements that were dear to him. Wilson's unforked tongue declares the resurrection of Jesus to be "a whopping lie." He credits Jesus with seeing, perhaps for the first time in history, the radical implications of the equality of all peoples, rich and poor.

Rita Nakashima Brock and Rebecca Ann Parker produced a strikingly original book, *Saving Paradise: How Christianity Traded Love of This World for Crucifixion and Empire* (Beacon Press, 2008). Reaching into art as well as doctrinal history, the authors search out an earth-loving Christianity that got lost beneath dry creeds and formulae and poisonous myths of sacralized violence. This book does justice to what we can know of Jesus and to the spirituality that nourished him.

Elaine Pagels tells a lot about the Jesus that got away in *Beyond Belief: The Secret Gospel of Thomas* (Random House, 2005). It was epochal when Thomas's fist-century gospel was rejected in favor of John. When John's take on things was enshrined and Thomas's denounced as heresy, this "decisively shaped—and inevitably limited—what would become Western Christianity."

Reza Aslan's *Zealot: The Life and Times of Jesus of Nazareth* (Random House, 2013) rehearses a lot of the critical scholarship on the life of Jesus of Nazareth and gives a good picture of the players and antagonists in Jesus' life. He effectively demythologizes Jesus, though his characterization of Jesus as Zealot is not broadly embraced by biblical scholars.

Garry Wills, in *Why Priests? A Failed Tradition* (Viking, 2013), does his usual careful scholarship on the clergification of the Jesus movement. He is and writes as a Catholic, though his well-researched findings on the borrowings involved in the formation of the church and on the central liturgy of Eucharist have challenged many in his Catholic fellowship.

The preexistence of Jesus, a divine person, born before all time is the topic of Karl-Josef Kuschel in *Born Before All Time?: The Dispute over Christ's Origin* (Crossroad, 1992), and is an exhaustive and exhausting study of how theology has handled this enigmatic construct of a person who existed eternally before he was born. He shows how the notion of preexistence has appeared in other contexts. There are grounds here for more radical conclusions than the author reaches regarding such postbiblical constructions as the "triune God." As in the tomes of Hans Kung, there is a hesitancy here to fully face the implications of the research presented, implications that cannot be reconciled with the orthodoxy of the councils.

With a sprightly style of writing, Robin R. Meyers, a well-informed pastor, takes on the challenges of bad theology functioning as a cover for hypocritical behavior in the Christian churches in *Saving Jesus from the Church: How to Stop Worshiping Christ and Start Following Jesus* (HarperOne, 2009). In my terms he is saying that many Christians are dogmatically orthodox moral heretics since certain legends are embraced with fervor while the moral challenge of the biblical epic is strategically bypassed. Alongside Meyers' book is *Jesus Before Christianity*, by the Dominican scholar Albert Nolan (Orbis Books, 1978).

In *The Illegitimacy of Jesus: A Feminist Theological Interpretation of the Infancy Narratives* (Harper & Row, 1987), Jane Schaberg addresses the early rumor of Jesus' possible illegitimacy. The book is more important than the rumor since it explores the infancy narratives. She does a sterling job showing that Mary's *Magnificat* in Luke's Gospel is not just a pious hymn without prophetic fire. Rather she shows why it has been called "one of the most revolutionary documents in all literature, containing three separate revolutions"— moral, social, and economic. In *Mary Magdalen Understood* (Continuum, 2006), Schaberg gives the lie to the many fanciful tales of Mary Magdalene.

Life After Death

In imagining life before birth and life after death, religious imagination shows its immunity to limits. Seeing birth as rebirth from a previous life is in the same genre. Imagining that death is illusory, only apparent, offers consolation to the bereaved and hope for all mortals. Its popularity is witnessed in the varied history of peoples and cultures. In *The Early History of Heaven* (Oxford University Press, 2006), J. Edward Wright shows how one's ascent into the heavens where the gods dwell was a common hope. Afterlife hopes take various poetic forms in ancient Sumer, Assyria, and Babylonia, and also very strongly in Christian and Islamic traditions. The variety in these traditions provide witness to their imaginative source. Christian heaven is sexless. Some Islamic views of postmortem paradise show no such inhibitions.

Philosopher Corliss Lamont goes after the illusion of immortality with gusto in his book by that name (*The Illusion of Immortality*, Continuum, 1990). With a supportive Introduction by John Dewey, Lamont uses science and reason to dispel afterlife hopes, but goes on to argue that this does not leave us bereft of moral motivation or a sense of meaning. Ethics in his view does not perish with immortality.

Resources for a Global Ethic

The common good is the matrix of all private good. Any nation that does not systematically meet the needs of the social whole becomes a failed state. The planet is now a failed planet. The actual state of the nations is anarchy; there is no supra-national authority to ensure the fair flow and distribution of goods and burdens. The result is that greed reigns. Justice, as Aquinas said, consists in sharing. In the absence of appropriate sharing, one-percentism ensues and the pyramid model with power and wealth at the pinnacle is the oppressive result, with nature itself as the first casualty. A global ethic to begin to address this ecological, demographic, economic, and political disaster is a matter of life and death.

The rampaging human community is not lacking in clear-eyed analyses of our global disease. On the ecological mess, see: Clive Ponting, *A Green History of the World: The Environment and the Collapse of Great Civilizations* (Penguin Books, 1991); Edward O. Wilson, *The Future of Life* (Knopf, 2002); Jared Diamond, *Collapse: How Societies Choose to Fail or Succeed* (Penguin Books, 2005); Larry L. Rasmussen, *Earth-Honoring Faith* (Oxford University Press, 2013); Harold Coward and Daniel C. Maguire, editors, *Visions of a New Earth: Religious Perspectives on Population, Consumption, and Ecology* (State University of New York Press, 2000); Daniel C. Maguire and Larry L. Rasmussen, *Ethics for a Small Planet* (State University of New York Press, 1998).

With a particular focus on the transfer of power from nations to corporations, David Korten spelled out the consequences in *When Corporations Rule the World* (Kumarian Press, 1995–1996). For another book that is a classic in detailing how the powerful can rape and destroy whole cultures and people, nothing is better or more graphic than *Open Veins of Latin America: Five Centuries of the Pillage of a Continent* by Eduardo Galeano (Monthly Review Press, 1997).

Permit me to single out one indispensable journal, *Monthly Review: An Independent Socialist Magazine.* This journal brings constant attention to the earth-wrecking deficiencies of archaic but still dominant economic and political patterns. No other journal is more relentlessly on target.

Jonathan Schell, in *The Unconquerable World: Power, Nonviolence, and the Will of the People* (Metropolitan Books, Holt, 2003), shows how the esteemed notion of "sovereignty" is a fallacy and a force for social disintegration. Schell points the way to a reshaping of the very concept of governance in a globalized world.

Two fine examples of "woman spirit rising" and a tough analysis of the flawed assumptions of the man-made world are Mary Elizabeth Hobgood's *Dismantling Privilege: An Ethics of Accountability* (Pilgrim Press, 2009) and Gloria Albrecht's *Hitting Home: Feminist Ethics, Women's Work, and the Betrayal of "Family Values"* (Continuum, 2002). Albrecht does surgery on the existing cultural practices that give elite men the power to dominate the course of social change in both public and private places. Any global ethic that does not cope with the male grip is condemned to superficiality. Showing that feminist scholarship is not only done by women, John Raines' book, *The Justice Men Owe Women: Positive Resources from World Religions* (Fortress Press, 2001) finds positive elements amid the sexism of world religions.

Have Christians been a help or a hindrance in all of this? The answer is yes! On the chronic military fever of our species, Roland Bainton made an indispensable contribution with *Christian Attitudes Toward War and Peace*, first published in 1960 by Abingdon Press. A companion volume that cries out for republication is Stanley Windass's *Christianity Versus Violence*, published by Sheed and Ward in 1964. Bluntly facing the downside of both the Bible and the Quran is Jack Nelson-Pallmeyer's *Is Religion Killing Us?* (Continuum, 2003). Alice Beck Kehoe's *Militant Christianity: An Anthropological History* (Palgrave Macmillan, 2012) shows how the militarism of the Christian right seeps into the broader culture. Add to this collection the penetrating book of Barbara Ehrenreich, *Blood Rites: Origins and History of the Passions of War* (Holt, 1997).

In getting to the historical roots of why Christians are the way they are, Dennis Nineham is a master guide. See his *Christianity Mediaeval and Modern* (SCM Press, 1993) and *The Use and Abuse of the Bible: A Study of the Bible in an Age of Rapid Cultural Change* (Macmillan Press, 1976).

What is sometimes called "the Catholic just war theory" (because Catholic scholars have labored long on it) got legs and is the most widely used and often misused tool in the ethics of war-making internationally. Properly understood it is a peacemaker's true friend since it puts the burden of proof on the war-maker, not the conscientious objector. I try to show what the just war theory really says in my short book, *The Horrors We Bless: Rethinking the Just War Legacy* (Fortress Press, 2007).

Aside from the biblical scholarship referenced earlier, certain works need special mention. Norman K. Gottwald's monumental *The Tribes of Yahweh: A Sociology of the Religion of Liberated Israel, 1250–1050 B.C.E.* (Orbis Books, 1985) is in a class by itself. Of similar distinction is Abraham Heschel's *The Prophets*, published as a single volume by the Jewish Publication Society of America in 1962.

No biblical scholar is more attuned to the poetic power of the Hebrew biblical authors than Walter Brueggemann. No scholar is better at showing the biblical poets' continuing contemporaneity. The poetry of early Israel shines bright with revolutionary colors in all his writings, but especially in *Journey to the Common Good* (Westminster John Knox Press, 2010). Similar praise is due his earlier work, *The Prophetic Imagination* (Fortress Press, 1978). See also his *Revelation and Violence: A Study in Contextualization* (Marquette University Press, 1986). Brueggemann uses God language but nontheists need not be put off unless they are unduly skittish, since a view of "God" as metaphor in this richly poetic literature makes disputes about whether there is a personal super-being unnecessary.

On the neglected and often buried defense of the power of non-violent resistance to all tyrannies nothing beats Walter Wink's four volumes from Fortress Press: *Naming the Powers: The Language of Power in the New Testament* (1984); *Unmasking the Powers: The Invisible Powers that Determine Human Existence* (1986); *Engaging the Power: Discernment and Resistance in a World of Domination* (1992); and *When the Powers Fail: Reconciliation in the Healing of Nations* (1998).

And last, but anything but least, is Thomas Cahill's boldly entitled and masterfully and beautifully written *The Gifts of the Jews: How a Tribe of Desert Nomads Changed the Way Everyone Thinks and Feels* (Anchor Books, Doubleday, 1998).

INDEX